A PRACT

TO BE

CONCENTRATION

A PRACTICAL GUIDE TO BETTER CONCENTRATION

Melvin Powers
author, "Dynamic Thinking"

Robert S. Starrett
author, "Find a Career in Medicine"

Published by
Melvin Powers
WILSHIRE BOOK COMPANY
12015 Sherman Road
No. Hollywood, California 91605
Telephone: (213) 875-1711 / (818) 983-1105

Printed by

HAL LEIGHTON PRINTING COMPANY
P.O. Box 3952
North Hollywood, California 91605
Telephone: (818) 983-1105

Library of Congress Catalog Number: 62-12886
Printed in the United States of America

ISBN 0-87980-120-4

CONTENTS

FOREWORD

In the last few years there has been a tremendous upsurge of adults seeking self-improvement. They are enrolled in courses of all kinds, and not a few of them are working for high school or college diplomas after many years of absence from the classroom. Many of these older students are finding it easier to learn than when they were younger while others are finding it harder.

It would be easy to say the difference in the learning ability of the two groups is a matter of basic intelligence or the degree of motivation, but this would be an oversimplification. Actually, motivation is strong in both groups, and the difference seems to lie in the ability to concentrate. Those experiencing difficulty usually say they were never able to concentrate, and many of them admit that this lack had a great deal to do with the brevity of their education.

It is no secret that knowledge cannot be obtained without concentration, yet millions of people blandly acknowledge they lack this prerequisite to learning. The expressions, "I just can't seem to concentrate" or "I never could concentrate" are so common they occasion very little comment. Indeed, many of those using these rationalizations sound as though they took a measure of pride in their deficiency. The implication by those who say they cannot concentrate is that they are suffering from a congenital condition beyond their control.

Nothing could be further from the truth. Anyone with normal intelligence, and that includes most of us, can learn to concentrate. But learning to concentrate must be preceded by intense intellectual curiosity, a burning desire to learn something about everything under the sun. It is in fostering this desire that our American educational system has broken down and the same thing can be said of the American home. Parents and teachers who make no effort to instill intellectual curiosity in a child will inevitably produce an adult who has no desire to learn.

The fact that you are reading this book indicates that you have developed at least a modicum of intellectual curiosity and wish to improve your concentrative powers so you can pursue your newly-awakened desire to learn. With this motivation, you have the basic ingredient for concentration. The rest can be learned.

Increasing your powers of concentration will do far more than help you in the accumulation of abstract ideas and the attainment of a higher cultural level. You will find that concentration leads to logical thought processes which will allow you to solve the daily problems that are now causing you stress and anxiety. For the first time you will have the leisure and confidence to explore all the avenues of interest which add so much to the lives of those you have envied for the richness of their talents. Talent, unlike genius, can be uncovered in any one who takes the trouble to try everything.

Undoubtedly, you have reached a point where you feel that your lack of concentration is a handicap and your inability to attain it is a constant frustration. This frustration is followed by feelings of self-deprecation resulting in even less ability to concentrate. A negative cycle is strengthened and perpetuated by each failure and when this pattern persists long enough the individual will stop making attempts to learn difficult material. The ego will not risk exposing itself to continual failure. The unconscious mechanism is that one's sense of adequacy will not be as adversely affected by avoiding mental effort as it will by trying and failing.

There is no need to continue this pattern, however. The ability to increase your powers of concentration is inherent. Desire and motivation to learn and the techniques in this book will bring out this latent asset. If you faithfully follow the instructions, you can confidently expect to achieve goals you have always thought were impossible for you. Best of all rewards will be the exciting new feeling of self-esteem which will follow your mental accomplishments.

ROBERT S. STARRETT

MELVIN POWERS

12015 Sherman Road
No. Hollywood, California 91605

Chapter 1

What You Should Know About Concentration

Most people profess to believe that the ability to concentrate is an inborn characteristic, as impossible to change as the general nature of their body structure or the color of their eyes. There is a great deal of evidence to indicate, however, that this is an unconscious rationalization or face-saving device which will not bear a searching and honest self-analysis. In a highly competitive world where one's resources are being constantly tried, it is comforting to be able to blame fate, heredity or circumstances for our short-comings rather than place the stigma where it belongs—on ourselves. Psychiatrists are familiar with this sort of rationalization which occurs spontaneously to save the ego. Unfortunately, this unwitting form of subterfuge, while it may offer a measure of comfort, does nothing to eradicate the problem.

We believe, along with the largest body of psychologists, that no one is born with the power to concentrate any more than one is born with a taste for exotic foods. It is an acquired characteristic and must be tended and nurtured

11

every day, but anyone with normal intelligence can acquire it.

It should be clear from the above that we believe nearly every person has the potential ability to concentrate, but it does not follow that every person will develop this latent power. There are a number of variables that determine whether this important asset to learning will ever become part of your mental equipment. The chief variable, as mentioned in the foreword, is intellectual curiosity. It has been said that those who would like to live to a ripe old age should "choose" their parents with care. This also holds true for those who would like to learn to concentrate intensely. If you have been stimulated since childhood to be curious about everything in your environment you will have no trouble in learning to concentrate. It will be almost as easy and automatic as breathing. If you do not have this sort of curiosity you will have to develop it. It is a prerequisite to learning and concentration.

Many other variables exert an effect on your ability to concentrate. The schools you attend, the curriculum, the teachers, your motivation and goals and your physical health are a few of them. These will be discussed in later chapters of this book.

The most important fact you must prove to yourself is that you *do* have the ability to concentrate. When you say that you have never been able to concentrate, what you are really saying is that you have never been able to concentrate in certain areas that you felt were beyond your mental powers. In reality, you have never even tried to concentrate in these areas. The truth is that concentration is a relative quality and it can be easy, difficult or impossible to develop according to the subject matter.

A good example of relativity in concentration can be made by comparing recreational and intellectual subjects. Consider the student who remarks that he cannot concentrate on his studies no matter how hard he tries, yet becomes so absorbed in watching a television program that he is oblivious to all around him. If it is a baseball game he is watching, he spontaneously, without effort, develops total recall for every play made during the game. Questioning would probably reveal that he knows the batting average of every player on his favorite team, and it is not unlikely that he knows similar statistics about every player in the league.

This same student may demonstrate equal facility in remembering football and basketball statistics, be up to the minute on the progress of twenty or more comic strips and be able to tell you all the details of a murder mystery he is reading. He keeps up with all these things with a zeal that would make him a top notch student in any field, yet he will tell you ruefully that he can scarcely remember the date of the War of 1812. Obviously, there is nothing wrong with his ability to concentrate. He has only to transfer his ability into more intellectual channels.

The above case plainly indicates that concentration is automatic when interest in a subject is high. The main difficulty, then, appears to be the development of interest in something the individual should learn, but is not willing to make the effort. He is not willing to make the effort because he is not motivated, and he is not motivated because of a lack in his environment. Somewhere along the line his interest in achieving high mental prowess or technical skills has been sidetracked by our modern desire to get everything the "easy way."

For many years our school curriculums have become more and more easy, and it is only recently that educators have begun to take a hard look at a school system which dispensed too many diplomas and not enough intellectual stimulation. The tendency is to make schooling much more difficult than it has been, but for those who attended under the old regime it will be too late. They will have to summon up the interest to help themselves without benefit of new teaching methods. This will require a great deal of self-discipline. If one is "getting by," the tendency is to leave things as they are.

We will assume at this point, because you are reading this book, that you have finally decided to do something about improving your powers of concentration. This is the first step, of course, but the mere fact that your interest has been awakened will not automatically result in the ability to concentrate. Starting at this late stage, it must be a learned process. The desire to drop something hard for something easy will plague your efforts, and the thoughts of previous failures will provide another variable which can cause discouragement, frustration and further failure.

It is well to remember here that forgetting is a normal part of everyday life. It is not necessary or even desirable that we remember every event and detail in our lives. Nature, for instance, has a way of helping us to forget unpleasant episodes. We think of the "good old days" as if nothing but pleasant things had happened during that time, but the fact is that those days were compounded of good and bad just like the present. But even though many things are "forgotten" by the conscious mind, nothing is forgotten by the subconscious. Every experience of our life is filed away in the subconscious and most of them can be recalled through the use of certain psychological processes. In learning to concentrate it is necessary that you recall successful attempts in learning rather than unsuccessful ones so that you are not adversely affected at the outset by a failure pattern.

People express their inability to concentrate in many different ways. Forgetting, absentmindedness, day dreaming, lack of interest and inattention, for example, are merely other ways of revealing a lack of concentration. Those who lack concentration usually choose a euphemism which bears less stigma than the specific term involved. The difference here is only in semantics.

Speaking semantically, it is necessary to point out that attention and concentration are not really the same thing. If, while reading this book, you are aware of surrounding sounds and vagrant thoughts, your attention is still basically on the text. Concentration, however, is measured by one's ability to shut out distractions and focus on the problem at hand.

There is a great deal of confusion about the real meaning of concentration. Many people think it is the ability to think solely about one single idea or object. A little experimenting should convince you that this is impossible. The amount of time the mind can concentrate exclusively on one idea is measured in seconds because other ideas, even though they be on the same subject, are constantly crossing the mind. William James, the famous Harvard psychologist, recognized this aspect of concentration when he said that it occurred whenever an idea, thought or objective "most completely" occupied the mind. In other words, he realized that nothing could completely occupy the mind. He had to qualify the word. In deep concentration there is an automatic shifting of attention to related subjects and the ability to fix your mind for long periods on a single thought is a myth.

To prove this, let us try an experiment. Try, if you can,

to concentrate on the first word in this paragraph, the word "To." You will instantly realize that it is impossible to separate the word completely from the surrounding words. As a matter of fact, the anatomical construction of the eye will make it impossible for you not to see, to some extent, every other word on the page. In addition to this, you will be aware of sounds, body feelings and a variety of associated or disassociated ideas going through your mind.

Perhaps you think the above example is unfair because you cannot help seeing the other words on the page, so let's make it easier for you to concentrate. Light a candle in a dark room and stare fixedly at it while trying to maintain a single thought. You will soon find a host of ideas chasing through your mind, be aware of bodily sensations and may even find yourself thinking about an entirely different subject. The Chinese have been using this method of fixating attention for centuries, but it is not recorded that any have achieved pure concentration for more than a few seconds and even this length of time is a conjecture.

Despite this distraction of attention, the word, object or thought you are trying to concentrate on will still be the main object of your attention. All distractions are considered marginal. The distractions are there and you are conscious of them but your attention is concentrated on the subject most of the time. Obviously, the more intensely you are able to fix your mind on the subject, the less you will be aware of the distractions. But it is well to remember that no matter how proficient you become at concentration, you will never be able to completely rule out distractions. The idea is to approach "pure" concentration as closely as possible, but your goal must be realistic. If you think that concentration means ruling out all distractions, you are foredoomed to failure. It might be added here that a good deal of the disappointments in this world are traceable to the fact that people set unrealistic goals for themselves, goals they can never hope to achieve. In the next chapter we will discuss the distractions you can do something about and those you will never be able to completely eliminate.

It has been stated previously that the only way you can learn to concentrate on something is to develop an interest in it. It becomes necessary, then, to ascertain how you can develop an interest in something that has not heretofore merited your attention. This does not seem so hard when you realize that almost all interests are artificial, not natural, and have grown from "small acorns." The boy engrossed with baseball was not born with this interest. He had to develop it. And his interest in the game increased in exact proportion to his increase of knowledge about the game. Briefly, if you wish to increase your interest in a desired subject, start off by securing some information about it. This small bit of information will inevitably lead you to a further desire for information. Isn't that the way all hobbies start?

Before going on to further illustrations of how an individual can increase his interest and concentration, it should be made clear that these two important qualities cannot be separated from the rest of the personality. Actually, gaining these assets requires the neophyte to develop a whole new concept of himself. The person who is unable to concentrate has, in reality, a personality problem which has resulted from continually thinking of himself as doomed to failure in almost all higher forms of mental endeavor. Trying to deal with the concentration problem without dealing with the individual's fundamental emotional feelings about himself will only lead to further failures.

The person who talks about his poor powers of concentration is really talking about his untrained mind, his lack of self-confidence, self-esteem and many other negative factors that underlie the symptom he mentions. And so, although the immediate objective is to increase the ability to concentrate, the long-range goal is to change the total personality which has been functioning inadequately. This requires a psychologically sound program and it cannot be accomplished by treating one symptom.

In today's highly competitive world, the victory goes to those who have the self-confidence to face every challenge. No challenge can be met if one's self-esteem is low. You must first imagine yourself being successful in all your endeavors before the goal can be attained. It is a well-known fact that if we think of something long enough and hard enough, it will tend to realize itself.

We have heard a great deal in the last two decades about the American dream, and we should remember that we are speaking of an ideal that first existed in the imagination and was then translated into goal-directed work. Our founding fathers built this nation by hard work but this work was preceded by a vision of themselves living in a land of plenty "from sea to shining sea." It is a successful vision of yourself that you must carry in the forefront of your mind at all times. There will be a great deal said about how you can acquire this successful image of yourself in later chapters.

We have stated that there is a great deal of alarm being expressed today about America's educational system. Business leaders and educators everywhere say that many of the modern generation cannot read with comprehension or write with clarity. Graduate students in law and medical schools often cannot spell well enough to make themselves clearly understood. Thomas M. Cooley II, dean of the

School of Law, University of Pittsburgh, recently called attention to a law student who finally confessed that he could not spell well enough to even look words up in a dictionary, and this is not an isolated case (A Law School Fights Graduate Illiteracy. *Saturday Review,* August 12, 1961). The graduate schools are blaming the colleges, the colleges are blaming the high schools and the high schools are blaming the grade schools for this state of affairs.

Recent additions of remedial courses to school curriculums show that educators know that something is wrong but there is a great deal of argument concerning what should be done. One thing is certain: Even remedial courses will be flunked if students have never learned to concentrate and study in the first place. The obvious mistake of educational institutions is that they assume that students, at some previous time, have acquired study habits that will allow them to complete the curriculum. That is why each division of learning blames the next lowest division and the lowest division blames the parents, the times and a host of assorted ills. It would be interesting to learn how many students who drop back to remedial courses ever catch up with their classmates and go on to become brilliant or even average students. We suspect the number would be very low.

Educational institutions are now busy adding courses to their curriculums but nearly all of them assume that students have somehow learned to concentrate, listen, read, write and take notes before taking these courses. What is really needed at all levels of education is a practical guide in learning to concentrate and study.

One factor often overlooked by parents, educators, business leaders and others in authority is that individuals must succeed in small things before they can succeed in larger ventures. President Eliot of Harvard, editor of the famous

"Five Foot Shelf" of books to aid adults in correcting their educational deficiencies, once stated that many failures in elementary school were due to the fact that students, at the beginning, were not given enough work at which they could succeed. Because of this, they never developed the feeling of success so necessary to confidence, self-esteem and the continuation of learning. We have already mentioned how important it is to be able to recall successes, not failures, and parents and schools should deliberately arrange to make children successful in the beginning so they will have the confidence to pursue higher goals. Even though you are an adult, you should arrange to start pursuing your new goal of concentration by doing things in which you can be successful.

This book will not offer you an easy system for "instant concentration." It will offer you a practical formula that has already helped innumerable students and adults at all levels of achievement. The technique involved is a relatively new and unorthodox one, but it operates on proved psychological processes. The validity of this method has been proved over a period of fifteen years, and the results have been extremely rewarding. In many cases, remarkable results have ensued and literally thousands of case histories indicate you may change your failure pattern for a success pattern if you apply yourself diligently to the methods which will follow.

The chapters that follow are designed specifically to help you develop your powers of concentration, but the general goal is to allow your personality to reach its highest potential. The information will embody the latest scientific and psychological findings in the fields of learning and concentration, and will tell you how to incorporate these findings into a workable formula for success.

Chapter 2

The Anatomy of Concentration

Learning to concentrate intensely enough to master difficult subjects requires the coordination of many dissimilar factors. Setting aside a certain time for study every day, for instance, is an important adjunct to learning, but it can be partially nullified if the studying is done in a physical environment which is incompatible with concentration. In this chapter, we will look at the mental and physical factors which play a part in concentration.

Before learning the psychological factors that affect concentration and learning, it is necessary to pay attention to your physical health. A feeling of well-being and abundant vitality induces a feeling of self-confidence while a "half-dead" feeling induces depression and the feeling that nothing is worth the trouble. Overcoming inertia is the most difficult problem you will face in settling down to hard study and concentration, and if it is further increased by lassitude and disinterest stemming from poor health, you will have a difficult time accomplishing anything.

History records some examples of outstanding geniuses who created immortal masterpieces in their fields despite precarious health, but we are not all geniuses and the average person finds poor health an almost insurmountable obstacle in the path of success. Only a fanatical belief that one has something important to do or say in the world can overcome the handicap of an ailing body. But there have always been—and always will be—some whose profound conviction of their destiny will override all physical restrictions, and nothing can stop them from succeeding. Actually, according to Alfred Adler, one of Freud's original students, these people succeed because of their physical limitations. He called this the theory of "organ inferiority" and said that people suffering from this deficiency overcompensated for it by applying themselves to their careers with unshakable purpose.

The above is mentioned to prove that nothing can really stop you if you wish to succeed, but it does not detract from what we have said about the average person being adversely affected by poor health. It is impossible to estimate how many people complain that aches, pains, fatigue and nervousness prevent them from applying themselves to things they would like to learn. But we all know such people and it is safe to say that many millions eliminate themselves from the race for success before it is well started because they lack the stamina to compete. They are bogged down in a morass of physical symptoms which effectually prevent them from starting any project. It matters little whether these symptoms stem from the mind or the body because psychosomatic illness (which is what people mean when they say, "It's all in your mind.") is just as painful or debilitating as illness caused by organic dysfunctioning. If you are one of those plagued with various symptoms which prevent you from even starting toward your goal, you would do well to seek competent medical and psychiatric advice. Millions of Americans blame their lack of drive on physical illness but the real culprit is their undisciplined emotions which have led to a crippling neurosis. Such a situation should always be considered by those who have "never been able to concentrate."

Other millions of individuals, however, are not operating at peak efficiency simply because they do not pay enough attention to sleep, proper diet and moderate exercise. In a nation surfeited with "entertainment," rich foods and a "push-button" environment which can virtually eliminate exercise, it is easy to take the path of least resistance and avoid the discipline necessary to health, both physical and emotional. Television, for instance, effectually prevents even an interchange of ideas during the long evening hours, but it is apparent that a great many Americans are addicted to this form of predigested "thought." Coronary disease continues to increase but overeating is so prevalent that every other American now suffers from overweight to some extent. The automobile has displaced walking to such an extent that those who indulge in it are considered eccentric or even suspicious. In the city of Beverly Hills, California, a post-prandial walk around the block can result in questioning by the police who believe this is a highly suspicious form of locomotion.

All of these things are mentioned here because we feel they all play a part in the complacency which has stifled true intellectual curiosity in this country for several decades now. It is reflected in our school system which has been most inadequate in preparing the average student for serious mental endeavor. It is true there is an upper echelon of thinkers who keep this nation at or close to the top in all fields, but it has not, at least until recently, been popular to learn things for the sheer joy of learning.

Fortunately, the picture is beginning to change and millions of young Americans are becoming motivated to learn, educators are agitating to change the school system and adults are enrolling in extension courses and branching out in many avenues of self-improvement. This is encouraging and the bright student in school as well as the "egghead" in adult life are gradually assuming their proper niche in American life.

Some of the factors we have mentioned as adverse to concentration and learning may properly be considered as distractions, and it is distractions that are the greatest enemies of those who wish to reach their highest potential in mental attainment. A distraction can be anything that diverts your attention from the subject at hand, and a good idea is to list everything that keeps you from studying or diverts your attention when you are studying. Systematically try to eliminate these distractions. In some cases you will not be able to do this, but aim at the irreducible minimum. All diversion of concentration is detrimental to concentration.

A large bone of contention at the present time between students and their parents is radio music which the former consider a necessary attribute to study. A musical background is considered of some help in raising the efficiency of production lines engaged in routine jobs, but it does not follow that this would be true of mental endeavor. Inasmuch as most of these students listen to popular vocal records, it should be obvious that there must be a splitting of attention. It is impossible to learn the words of a song or listen to a melody and still give your whole attention to your lessons, and the theory that the radio helps you concentrate is fallacious. Students who study in this manner learn despite this distraction. Their grades would greatly improve if the radio were eliminated.

Adults, too, should seek the quietest spot possible, away from the radio and television and the comings and goings of the rest of the family. People walking in and out of a room, even if they say nothing, cause a constant shifting of attention. Have you ever been in a large office given over to typing? If you have, you have undoubtedly noticed how all the other girls turn to watch when one of them gets up and leaves the room. In this case it is not very serious because their eyes can instantly return to the line they are copying, but if you are engaged in trying to grasp an idea, such distractions may force you to start over again each time you are interrupted.

The best way to concentrate is to set aside one certain room equipped with everything you will need during the study period. Very quickly this room will become associated with concentration and learning, and this will automatically facilitate your work. It will become a helpful habit.

It has been said that the human personality is a collection of habits. If good habits predominate, we are apt to be successful and if they do not, we tend to fail. Nearly all our actions are determined by habit, and it is necessary that we cultivate those habits that will aid us. Thus, in learning to concentrate, the individual should develop as many habits as possible that can be associated with the act of concentration.

Developing associative habits can be carried as far as the individual wishes. The authors are acquainted with a well-known writer who, for thirty years or more, has donned the same jacket when he begins a new book. There is a definite association in his mind between wearing the jacket and his ability to create written words. He knows, of course, that the jacket itself does not help him to write, but he has associated it with writing for so long that it has become indispensable. Some writers say that lighting a cigarette always starts a flow of words when they are blocked, while others say running their fingers tentatively over the typewriter keys establishes communication with their ideas. The main thing is to establish as many habits as possible that can be related to thinking and learning.

Consider the chair in which you are going to sit while trying to concentrate. Is it a chair you associate in your mind with mental relaxation or napping? If it is, you would be wise to use one that you can eventually associate with concentrated mental effort. This does not mean that the chair should be uncomfortable but merely that it should not be the overstuffed or reclining type. It does not follow that a Spartan-like environment will inevitably lead to good scholarship. It is likely, in fact, that Abraham Lincoln could have studied a great deal better with an electric light than he did by the light of a fireplace.

If your concentration must result in something written, always use the same method of recording your thoughts. Some writers say they can only write in longhand while others complain of a paucity of ideas unless they use a typewriter. Erle Stanley Gardner, the famous mystery story writer and creator of Perry Mason, is one of the growing group who states he is at his best while using a dictating machine. The point here is that it doesn't make a great deal of difference what you associate with concentration and learning so long as it becomes a habit which will help you achieve your goal.

One of the greatest drawbacks to concentration is the feeling that nothing can be learned unless it is "pleasurable." If this is what you believe, inertia will surely prevent you from even starting most projects which might be considered intellectual. The way to prevent this is to "start easy." Your interest and pleasure in a certain subject is in exact ratio to the amount of information you have about it, and it follows that the more you learn the more you want to learn. Actually, the term "pleasurable" is relative. It may not be precisely pleasurable to memorize the fact that the sun is 93,000,000 miles from the earth, but one can take pleasure from the fact that one has learned it. More importantly, this small bit of information will lead to a desire to know more about this subject. It should also be apparent that memorizing this information will allow you to establish a success pattern. Unless you are successful right from the start, you will not have the desire to continue any form of learning. For this reason, it is a good idea to start each day's study with material that can be easily mastered, progressing to more difficult material as you "warm up." This is what the track athlete does as he jogs slowly around the track loosening up for the race soon to ensue.

You may have read that Erle Stanley Gardner is able to dictate three stories at once, switching from one story line to another without ever losing the thread of his separate plots. In doing this, Mr. Gardner is utilizing the psychological truth that one's interest in something can be renewed by resting or switching to another subject for a few moments. In studying, it is better to switch subjects than rest, however, because starting to study again after a rest will again require a warm-up period. We know many good students who use this psychological aid.

We mentioned at the start of this chapter that a certain time every day should be set aside for study and concentration. The purpose of this is to establish yet another habit pattern. It may be that you, at present, do not want to study or concentrate any more at one time of the day than another, but this can be changed. You can learn to associate a certain hour or hours with study just as you associate a certain hour or hours with recreation or eating. If you have always eaten lunch at noon, you will always be hungry at that hour and there are psychological as well as physiological reasons for your hunger pangs.

The most important psychological aid to concentration and study is motivation, but it is not the first step in the learning process. You cannot become motivated unless you first have a desire or wish to do something. This desire can lead to motivation and eventually to the wish-fulfillment which is your goal. Interest also precedes motivation. Without interest you cannot be motivated and without motivation you cannot do anything well.

Advanced educators know that creating a desire is the first step in making a good student and they instill these desires by showing what the goal or end result will be. Millions of students, for instance, have difficulty in becoming motivated to learn mathematics, yet many of them dream of becoming astronauts, jet pilots, bridge builders, electronic engineers or a famous figure in some allied field. Once they realize they cannot enter these fields without knowledge of higher mathematics, they can be strongly motivated. It only requires keeping the goal always in mind. Think in terms of your goals and you will be anxious to take the steps leading to them.

The thing to remember about goals is that they must be realistic. You may have a desire to be an ambassador to a foreign country, but if you have no facility in languages, you must either develop this facility or forget about your desire. The same is true of history, sociology, civics and political science if one is contemplating a career in which politics is involved.

The Anatomy of Concentration

Making money is a desire which most people acquire early in life. This is a very normal desire despite all the talk about how materialistic America has become, and that the amassing of money is its sole preoccupation. It can be said of money that it provides the strongest motivation of all, and if you were to remove the incentive of money, very little would be accomplished. As Veblen pointed out in *The Theory of the Leisure Class,* this is not all to the good, but you need not be ashamed if financial success is your chief goal. Generally, to become a financial success you will have to learn many things not directly connected with making money and these will be of intrinsic value. But there will be very few things you learn which cannot, in some way, be exploited for the purpose of making money. A student who studies Spanish because he loves the language may suddenly find an opening in an import-export business which exactly suits the talent he never intended to commercialize.

In mentioning the above, we are thinking of the person who says, "I don't see any point in concentrating on this subject. I'll never have any use for it." This may be specifically true in some cases but it is never generally true. One never knows when one's interest in something may become so intense that the whole course of one's life will be changed. A good share of certified public accountants took their first accounting course in high school thinking it might be of some help in businesses they contemplated.

The fact is most individuals limit their goals by limiting their knowledge, and they pursue the same humdrum path every day without ever knowing their lives could have been enriched by seeking to learn something about everything. If you will make it a point to learn a little about all the wonderful fields of endeavor today, you will inevitably find you will want to learn more. It is not necessary to be an expert in order to enjoy a certain subject. Most people who are referred to as "knowledgable" are not experts in all the subjects they pursue. But they know enough to be interested and interesting.

Far too many individuals feel they are not up to learning some of the things they wish to learn. Even some of those who have gone from wish to motivation to goal still feel that the course of study is too difficult for them. "I never did learn easily," they say ruefully. This, of course, brings us to self-confidence. Simply remember that most intellectual subjects in the world are so constructed that they can be understood by those of normal intelligence. The author of the subject may have been a genius, but he will not key his exposition of his subject only to other geniuses. Einstein was a genius, but you do not have to be a genius to understand the meaning of $E = mc^2$.

At the risk of repetition, we will state that a lack of self-confidence usually stems from the fact that you have not been successful in early endeavors. Either you have been given or have chosen work too advanced. It is absolutely necessary that you gain self-confidence by finding some field of mental endeavor in which you can be successful at the start and work through to more difficult material in easy stages. Start with 2×2 rather than $E = mc^2$.

In later chapters of this book, you will find many special techniques of concentration which will help you achieve your goals. In the meantime, consciously seek enough information about some subject to arouse your curiosity and interest. Remember that the anatomy of concentration is built on wishes, interests, motivations and goals.

Chapter 3

Psychological Factors in Concentration

Improving your ability to concentrate requires the formation of new thinking and behavior patterns. It may be that the individual with faulty concentration has inefficient study habits and a negative attitude in regard to his ability in these areas. Because of his inability, he is convinced his lack of facility in concentration is congenital. Many times he will give up attempting anything that requires concentration because he feels it is futile to try to improve.

The purpose of this chapter is to help you start building constructive attitudes and habits that will lead to better concentration and the attainment of goals that are impossible for you at present. You will find the learning process a rich and rewarding experience.

It is assumed you have a genuine desire to pursue a course of study, but have never been able to get started because of internal and external interferences and distractions which have diverted you from your plan. Undoubtedly, these barriers to concentration have served to destroy your intention to study and you never find yourself "in the mood" for anything that requires mental application. Individuals in this predicament never fail to find all sorts of reasons why they must postpone or give up study projects. Very few of these reasons are valid and the first step is to stop deceiving yourself. Avoiding a problem does not solve it and only strengthens your feeling of inadequacy.

The feeling of inadequacy is what prevents you from trying to overcome inertia, and it is absolutely essential that you develop counter feelings of worth and self-esteem. All of the suggestions and techniques in this book will be worthless unless you have a feeling deep within you that you will be successful at anything you try. This positive self-image is the most important aid to concentration and learning.

Despite the jeers directed at positive thinking books by pseudo-intellectuals, the fact remains that positive thinking is utilized by all successful persons. Call it what you will, no one can deny its importance in any endeavor. We are going to discuss how you can best utilize this philosophy in combination with other techniques to achieve goals that you seek. This is in line with the newest psychological belief that all therapy must be goal-oriented and -directed. Perhaps you have not thought of a learning and concentration program as therapy, but that is the correct term for any program that seeks to improve the mental and emotional reactions of the individual.

It is well to remember that one does not spontaneously begin to concentrate simply because a superficial attempt is made to think positively. Positive thinking and end results are attained only when the self-image is truly changed and the mechanics of utilizing suggestions are understood.

To understand how positive thinking can affect your self-image, it is best to start with the effect of negative thinking because you are more familiar with the process of downgrading yourself. For example, haven't you always accepted your own statements that you can't concentrate properly, can't keep your attention from wandering, can't easily comprehend reading material and can't keep distractions from diverting you? Haven't you, through repetition, convinced yourself that these statements are valid? Such statements, whether verbalized or not, have a profound effect on your ability to concentrate and study.

More than likely these statements about yourself have been true to some extent, but constant repetition has increased their ill effects. This is because everything you think about yourself filters into your subconscious mind which does not question, doubt, analyze or dispute the millions of impressions it receives. The constant feeding of negative opinions about yourself into the subconscious mind has a strong effect on your conscious activities. If negative opinions are reinforced long enough, the individual loses all power for constructive action.

It should be obvious that the image you have of yourself determines to a large extent how you will go about solving life situations. If you have faulty powers of concentration, this image of yourself becomes factual and fixed. Eventually you become convinced nothing can be done about it. You feel inferior to people who learn easily, but you seek to hide the fact from yourself by avoiding situations that will test your mental ability. Unfortunately, this ostrich-like attitude neither solves the problem nor changes your inner picture of yourself.

The power of a positive attitude can be remembered by thinking back to your school days. You will recall you always received the highest grade in the subject you liked and which you felt you could master. Conversely, your poorest grade was always in the subject you disliked and which you undertook with trepidation and premonitions of disaster. Obviously, your positive attitude was helpful. Your confidence that you would find the work easy was the basis of your success.

Developing the ability to concentrate and learn is a matter of harnessing the latent characteristics that everyone possesses. After all, poor students do become good students, and those who are successful in certain areas of achievement become proficient in areas where it was thought they had no aptitude. These changes are possible because the individual changes his feelings about himself and translates them into purposeful action. Our theme is that the initial impetus for improving your concentration must come from a changed attitude and increased self-esteem.

This system sounds easy but merely telling yourself that you are confident and will be able to achieve your goals will not change the situation immediately. Actually, a complete reconstruction of one's psyche is essential. This necessitates a substitution of good habit patterns for the ones that have been handicapping you, a belief that you can overcome your mental shortcomings and a willingness to test yourself by facing your problem.

The willingness to test yourself in learning situations depends on how completely you accept the dictum that you have the same potential ability as anyone else, barring a small group of especially endowed individuals. The gifted person will always excel, but it is to the average person that this book is directed. Mental prodigies are rare and if you would like to learn how they differ from the average person you should read *Mental Prodigies* by Fred Barlow.

If you will accept the fact that most of us have approximately the same intellectual capacity, you will have to agree that the real problem is in learning how to develop it. Of course, the ideal time for this development is in childhood, but if this was not the case you must believe it can be developed later by systematic practice.

The child is stimulated to be curious about everything in his environment by the intervention of his parents, but you will have to develop this quality by yourself. If you will think of all the things on the contemporary American scene that you know nothing about, you will realize there is no lack of subjects to attract your interest. How much do you know about literature, art, science and music? The cultivated person knows something about all of them and finds his knowledge opens new horizons and enriches his life.

Persons who have been so lacking in curiosity that they have never tried to learn anything difficult are in some ways better off than those who have tried and failed. Failure is a traumatic experience that can leave permanent scars unless the individual takes steps to learn the principles of success. These persons must start on the road back to confidence and self-esteem by being successful at something from the very beginning. Outstanding teachers recognize this need by starting chronic failures on something they are certain to master. If you are an adult and setting your own pace, do not try to learn more at the beginning than you can readily assimilate. Being successful from the start will give you the lift you need to conquer difficult subjects later on.

The importance of setting initial tasks you feel you can master cannot be overestimated. Newspapers frequently report student suicides in which the triggering factor has been poor grades. Such students fall so far behind they feel the struggle is hopeless. These, of course, are exceptional cases but many cases of depression are due to repeated failures which reduce self-esteem to the extinction point.

Remedial classes and adult classes where individuals of

similar educational backgrounds are grouped together are an excellent way of building up confidence and self-esteem because they usually backtrack to the point where contact with learning was lost. The element of competition is also important. Motivation increases when you test yourself against others although competition can be devastating if your thinking is still rooted in the old failure pattern.

Most persons starting a program of self-improvement which involves changing the self-image are fearful that they cannot visualize themselves as successful. "How," they ask, "can I see myself concentrating when it is something I have never been able to do?" It is necessary at this point to remember that every successful person has visualized himself as famous long before it became a reality. The actor dreams of becoming a star, the intern sees himself as a prominent physician, and the baseball rookie sees himself as a great pitcher or home run slugger. They are so obsessed with their ambition that it tends to spontaneously realize itself.

Being able to see the end result helps individuals overcome any obstacles that beset them along the path to their goals. Obstacles to such persons do not become road blocks but stepping stones to success. Opposition only strengthens their ability to weather each successive challenge. The proof of this can be seen all around us in the lives of those who have achieved success. Very few people reach their goals without overcoming obstacles which would defeat those less motivated.

One of the greatest psychological aids is a genuine interest in the subject to be mastered. Even though you have failed in previous attempts to learn in a certain field, the fact remains that you still have more aptitude for some things than others. Some of the unhappiest people in the world are those who tried to become successful in fields for which they had no inclination or interest. Parents are many times to blame for this. The boy who dreams of becoming a doctor is told he must study engineering. Or the youth who sees himself as a famous trial lawyer is admonished to become a business man. Frustration and failure usually result when individuals pursue goals not in keeping with their interests.

If you have no particular interest in anything of an intellectual nature, such an interest must be generated. It was stated in the first chapter that developing a genuine interest in a subject must be preceded by a certain amount of information about it. This is based on the well-known fact that an adult's interests are almost entirely artificial. They depend on life experiences, goals, responsibilities and desires.

Learning a little bit about something usually whets the appetite to learn more. Collecting stamps or coins is a good example of this principle. Acquiring the first unusual stamp or coin begins a chain reaction which can result in an all-consuming passion. Interest grows with each new bit of knowledge about the subject. In some cases the individual becomes so absorbed in the subject that he decides to make it a business rather than a hobby. Dealers in coins and stamps are enthusiasts who decided to spend all their time in the area of their chief interest.

One of the authors is well acquainted with a brilliant attorney whose whole life was changed when he took a course in torts as part of his studies in business administration. He became so interested in legal cases of civil wrongs that he switched to law school and graduated near the top of his class. He remembers his interest was aroused by the first case he read and this interest has continued to grow with the years.

37

One important thing to remember about interest is that not having it has probably prevented you from remembering most of the things you have studied. It is possible to read volume after volume about various subjects and remember practically none of it unless you are interested in what you are reading. This is a basic cause of failure at all levels of education. The student who reads an assigned chapter in history and remembers nothing about it has never developed an interest in this important subject. It is likely that the teacher never introduced the subject in an interesting fashion, but it is also likely the student somehow has come to think that all learning must be associated with pleasure right from the start.

It is a fallacy to believe that you can only learn those things that are pleasurable from the start. Like interest, pleasure only comes when you have gained enough knowledge and facility in a subject to do something with it. Keeping the goal always in mind will give you the original impetus to overcome the procrastination which affects everyone when a start must be made in a difficult area of learning.

The desire to withdraw from any form of mental endeavor which appears to be too difficult or not conducive to "fun" is well known to large business firms. They make their executive training programs compulsory and make the trainee's achievement of his goals contingent on his success in learning all phases of the business. Of course, those who are afraid of the responsibilities of executive positions are allowed to plod along in routine jobs.

This brings us to the fact that many people are psychologically unprepared to make important decisions. Their self-confidence has been shattered by early failures and they avoid situations which will require them to use judgment and logic. Such persons constitute the bulk of America's working force, and they apparently have no desire to rise higher than routine tasks. They trade the chance to advance for the security they feel in doing something at which they cannot fail. It is true somebody must do routine work but we assume that readers of this book wish to rise above their present station, not only economically but socially and culturally as well.

Those persons on whom no outside pressure is exerted to improve themselves must become "self-starters." This is difficult and requires great self-discipline, particularly if they are "getting by" without too many penalties being exacted. The high wages obtained for workers by labor unions and the general increase of wages in all fields have taken away some of the incentive which workers had when their future was entirely up to them. Protection of employees from piratical employers was and still is necessary, but our conformist culture tends to inhibit the drive of those who are individualistic.

Unfortunately, individualism is waning in all areas of American life. The desire to conform to the ideas and actions of one's peer group is, of course, very strong in most people. In young people, for instance, not being a member of the "gang" is a social catastrophe, and is tantamount to being banished to Siberia. They will do anything to gain acceptance by the group of their choice and willingly accept all the opinions and ideas of the group as their own. Most of them do not want to think in a way that will stamp them as "different."

Conformity for its own sake is part of childhood, but an adult with a healthy self-image and the ability to think for himself should never accept ideas or opinions simply because they have been adopted by a large group of people or been expressed by one or another of our many mass mediums of communication. The fact that something has been printed or broadcast does not necessarily make it so, and does not constitute true validation. Opinions or ideas for an individual should only become valid after he has subjected them to the higher processes of reason and logic.

Many viewers of the American scene have expressed concern with the growth of conformity in our culture, pointing out that it usually takes a radical departure from old ideas and methods to accomplish necessary changes in both the individual and the nation. The so-called organization man who stifles all personal feelings to conform with the feelings of the organization is a good example of the cultural sterility that results when all individualism is subordinated to the group. One has only to look at television commercials to see the effect of the "party line" on the creative efforts of the individual.

It is the authors' hope that this little excursion off the beaten path of the book will encourage you to weigh and analyze all ideas before you accept them as your own. With the proper amount of confidence and self-esteem, you need never accept an opinion just because it has been expressed by a group or medium of communication. Your newly awakened ability to concentrate and learn will furnish you all the tools you need to make up your own mind and not accept the pre-digested thoughts of others. Two books, *The Lonely Crowd,* by David Riesman and *The Organization Man,* by William F. Whyte, deal strongly with the subject we have just discussed.

A great many people who bemoan their lack of concentration also speak of their poor memory. It is no accident that these two negative qualities are usually mentioned together. They are merely different aspects of the same problem. The fact is that people fail to remember because they never knew what they were studying in the first place or they "disremember" purposely at an unconscious level. Obviously, you cannot remember something you skimmed over superficially, but forgetting on purpose happens psychologically because there is something unpleasant about what should be remembered.

Freud, the great exponent of the unconscious mind, postulated a theory of why people forget on purpose. It was his contention, for example, that people forget names of people with whom they have had unpleasant relations. One would think the opposite might be true, but his theory has been proved many times. In the same way you tend to forget those things for which you do not have a sincere love, and the end result may be that you may forget mathematical formula, dates in history, the conjugation of Latin verbs, etc. Psychologically you have not prepared yourself to remember these things because you have not summoned up sufficient interest, motivation or goals.

We have mentioned some of the psychological factors that affect concentration and learning. As you begin your program of self-improvement you may find many other psychological factors that affect your attitudes toward learning. Do not rationalize or practice self-deception when faced with negative factors. A direct frontal attack on your problems will usually result in their eventual disappearance.

Chapter 4

Use Your Subconscious for Better Concentration

This chapter title, at first glance, may arouse a bit of confusion as to how the subconscious mind can be used for such a conscious pursuit as concentration. However, although it sounds contradictory, closer examination will prove otherwise.

The latest thinking in regard to the functioning of the subconscious is that it can be compared to a goal-striving servo-mechanism. The human brain, nervous system and muscular system are a complex servo-mechanism, which means that the human mind can act as an automatic goal-seeking machine which steers its way to a goal by the use of feedback data and stored information, automatically correcting all errors. Our sense organs keep us informed when we are on the right track (positive feedback), and when we are "off course" it is corrected by negative feedback. It is clear here that the human brain has many similarities to a computer which solves problems in seconds and is continually corrected by negative feedback.

It is likely that everything we do is regulated by an automatic mechanism. All we have to do, for example, to pick up a cup of coffee is to have the desire. The goal has been chosen and your subconscious, because of years of conditioning, automatically corrects the course of your hand to your mouth. A baby, with very little conditioning, makes many ludicrous errors as it tries to lift a cup to its mouth. Once it has performed the maneuver successfully, however, it will be "remembered" in the subconscious for future use.

We know that the mathematical genius uses his subconscious mind to solve complex mathematical problems in an incredibly short period of time. The information is fed to the subconscious, is worked on automatically and the answer reported back to the conscious mind. Everyone does this to some extent in solving mathematical problems or problem solving in general.

There is a great deal of difference, however, between a human being and a computer. A computer is fed just enough negative feedback to correct its mistakes, but not enough to inhibit its function altogether. In other words, the function of negative feedback is to modify responses, not to stop them. Obviously, we cannot progress toward our goals without negative feedback, but we must be careful not to administer this corrective procedure too liberally.

Excessive negative feedback may cause the individual to become so inhibited that he is unable to make a proper response to any stimuli. We have all seen persons whose inhibitions are so strong that they are afraid to venture in any direction. For that reason we say excessive negative feedback and inhibition are identical.

A good example of what we are talking about might be the man who is rowing a boat toward a far shore and is using a large pier as a landmark. Because he is not facing the landmark, he will have to turn every few moments to correct his direction, but he does not stop rowing just because he is off course. He makes his correction and continues toward his objective.

This brings out the fact that negative feedback should always be more or less at the subconscious level and done automatically. The individual who is consciously too critical of himself may worsen his condition rather than improve it. In your course of self-improvement, you must avoid too much conscious self-criticism and concentrate on a long-range program which allows your subconscious to help do the work.

The thing to remember is that mistakes and failures are necessary steps to success in the learning process. You make progress by continually correcting your mistakes until you have hit on a successful pattern. Once you have found a successful pattern you must try to forget all about past mistakes and concentrate on the successful pattern until it is automatic. Remember, the operation of the subconscious is always automatic and it responds according to the information it receives. Positive thoughts are necessary because the subconscious actually reflects our conscious thinking, our environment and all our experiences. It is a synthesis of our experiential background whether it is remembered or forgotten by the conscious mind.

The importance of positive thoughts is clear when you know that the subconscious does not have the power to change negative thoughts to positive thoughts. It accepts and stores all types of information and suggestions as factual. When answers are needed, it provides them according to what it has "learned."

No automatic mechanism can function unless it has a goal and this is true of humans. It is extremely important to have a goal even though you originally do not know any way to achieve it. Do not worry about the means. If you think in terms of goals, the means usually will be forthcoming automatically. You will not know what these means will be in advance because the subconscious will not present solutions until there is a need. There will not be a need until you choose your goals.

Once you program constructive thoughts into your subconscious, your automatic guidance system will help steer you to your destination. The technique consists of two fundamentals: First, you must visualize yourself exactly the way you wish to be, possessing those powers of concentration that you earnestly seek; second, you must experience the results of this programming. Seek to constantly reenforce this new automatic reaction pattern. You can also think of it as establishing an automatic conditioned response.

When you achieve the ultimate results from using your subconscious for better concentration, studying or anything else, your powers of concentration will actually be effortless. The built-in guidance system will be working perfectly. When something interferes with the proper functioning of the subconscious, you will know it immediately and it will be corrected by negative feedback. Do not think of negative feedback as the same as negative thoughts. The former is helpful and the latter is disastrous.

Your initial efforts to concentrate will require a certain mental set which will encompass all your goals and aspirations. It is a technique which should be practiced every day so that the means to your ends have a chance to spontaneously emerge. There is a certain amount of mental discipline that you will need to muster.

As you visualize yourself concentrating properly, this impression is fed back into your subconscious making a favorable, successful response pattern which is remembered (stored) for future use. When you actually begin to concentrate at whatever task you earnestly desire, the stimulus is automatically acted upon by the subconscious and it duplicates and translates into results that which was previously imagined. It does this because it is responding and functioning to learned, remembered, programmed or conditioned information.

The triggering stimulus for proper concentration need not be the actual undertaking of the problem itself, but the intense desire to reach your goal. As soon as this happens, it puts into motion favorable psychological factors which automatically help you. It is similar to thinking about a pleasant experience that you know will happen. We enjoy the anticipation of spending a pleasant vacation, weeks and months before the actual time. If it's something special we are to do, the vibrant anticipatory emotions can have an uplifting effect upon our entire being.

It should be clear that your inadequate powers of concentration can be improved. It requires seeing the end result of your increased powers of concentration, seeing yourself actually concentrating, trying to capture the feeling of concentrating perfectly, and, most importantly, creating a new mental image of yourself by using your God-given powers of imagination which we all possess and which we can all use exceedingly easily. It is the use of the imagination which is our vehicle for successful results. Who among us cannot picture himself as successful? Doesn't this image automatically bring wonderful and exhilarating feelings? Try this experiment. Picture yourself, this moment, as already having achieved whatever you desire. Put down this book, close your eyes and dwell on this image for a few moments. Did you note something happening to you? If you didn't, you'll be able to feel this experience with a bit of practice.

We can all get our subconscious to function as an automatic, success-seeking servo-mechanism. An interesting psychological truism is that a person invariably responds to any situation as he imagines he should respond. It is to our advantage that the subconscious cannot distinguish between a real or imagined experience. We not only react to concrete situations but to what we think and believe is really so or to what we want to believe is so.

The writers of this book recently had an interesting experience which will point out an example of this type of thinking. At an informal party of friends, the host had hired an entertainer who makes his livelihood at parties by evaluating people at a glance and telling them his impressions as to what type of person the individual is. This is done in a friendly and jovial manner so that no one is embarrassed and everyone can hear and enjoy his impressions. After this was done for one woman, your authors happened to discuss one particular woman's "analysis" with two other women—one who liked the "analysand" and one who disliked her. The two women gave completely different interpretations to what was said and "swore" that the "analyst" did or did not make certain statements. Our suggestions as to what was really said were disregarded and we walked away leaving the argument still in progress. We often hear or see that which we want to see or hear.

Here, then, is our key. It depends on changing your mental image, substituting self-esteem for self-deprecation. Your inability to concentrate properly is a result of your own images, conscious or subconscious, and is the first step in fully understanding and doing something about the problem. Using your imagination affords you the opportunity of instilling these new attributes in your conscious and subconscious being. These impressions will form new engrams that will have a beneficial effect because, as we have pointed out, the subconscious cannot distinguish between a real or imaginary experience. It will be as though you had really concentrated perfectly in a given situation. The use of this visual imagery technique will help you in achieving the type of concentration ability that you seek. It is done by activating your creative success mechanism within your subconscious.

You will note that we have not stressed the use of will power in accomplishing your task. You have already tried this approach with seemingly unsuccessful results. If it had worked the way you wanted, you would not be reading this book. It is evident that it requires something more than just will power. The fallacy in using will power is that you consciously put too much emphasis on your unsuccessful concentration experiences. You proceed to study, your mind starts to wander, you remember a previous unsuccessful attempt and you convince yourself all over again of the validity of your concentration problem. As a result, your mental set is not conducive to improvement and further efforts only prove frustrating.

Success in using visual imagery lies in the uncritical acceptance of the constructive suggestions by the subconscious. As you practice this technique every day, the results become cumulative. The formula we have been advocating is sound and scientific and will work for you. Your problem started as a result of irrational interpretations of unsuccessful attempts to concentrate. It can be solved by a rational constructive attitude. Perhaps the prime factor is to stop thinking you have poor powers of concentration and shortcomings. Just begin to believe that you are going to improve your powers of concentration and whatever you do, don't dwell on your past failures or inadequacies in any area of your life. Making mistakes, experiencing failure and mistakes in judgment are all part of the process of development and maturing. The important consideration is to try to profit by these experiences and not let them bind you to a failure pattern. Most people never fully use their creative abilities because they have an inadequate self-image. They don't feel that they can do as well as someone else or feel that they don't deserve to be successful because of their own guilt feelings in regard to some situation in their lives. Their not becoming successful or fully developing their latent talents and abilities becomes a means of self-punishment and a re-enforcement of their own prophecy of defeat.

The catalyst in using visual imagery is your imagination, enthusiasm, and a sincere desire for a change. Merely mouthing and following the specific instructions for instilling these new feelings in your subconscious without the help of enthusiasm and zest is useless and a complete waste of time. You must give yourself to this technique with a deep conviction that it is going to work and that you will devote the time and energy needed in the procedure. This technique will be spelled out in the next chapter. It is quite elementary that a strong positive emotion can overcome a strong enervating emotion. For example, the man who suffers from a headache completely "forgets" about it when confronted by the fact that he has lost his wallet.

A poor concentration quotient can represent a strong self-destructive emotional reaction. If we assume that this statement is correct, it doesn't imply that it must remain so. Your reading this book is indicative that you have already generated enough desire to do something about it. It follows that you also believe you can do something about your problem. You have taken the first step in destroying the belief or image that you have congenitally poor powers of concentration. This belief has been self-perpetuating for too long a period of time.

As you begin to rely on your subconscious, it will help solve many of your problems. The concert pianist does not think about how he is going to strike every note in the composition he is playing. He sets the mood and relegates most of the interpretation and playing to his subconscious mind. Improving your concentration ability is something quite analogous to this. Once you have created the proper mood within yourself, good concentration becomes effortless because your subconscious is absorbing, categorizing and filing that which is to be learned. In other pursuits it is not concerned with the mechanics of the endeavor but with the end result. You could reasonably expect to become a good pianist with practice and you can expect to cultivate and develop your powers of concentration in the same way. It will come as you progressively experience successful attempts at concentration. As you continue, you will automatically get the "feel" of proper concentration. It is similar to an athletic team or individual having a "lucky streak." You know what happens when a team gets "hot," This same thing will happen when you begin to experience some success in concentration. The next chapter will give you the procedure for implementing what we have discussed in this chapter.

Chapter 5

The Technique for Developing Your Powers of Concentration

In the last chapter we discussed the functioning of the subconscious mind and its importance in developing better powers of concentration. We also suggested several ways of looking at the problem of concentration. Whichever way you choose, it will help you in developing and implementing better concentration. Your problem now is to reach your subconscious and inculcate the constructive suggestions, thoughts and images that we have discussed so that they become an integral part of your entire being.

The subconscious mind can best be influenced and controlled when the individual is in a state of complete relaxation, reflection, or meditation. It can then be directed and mastered. We suggest, therefore, that two periods each day be set aside for the purpose of influencing the subconscious through controlled suggestion. These periods need only be for ten minutes. The last period should be at night when you are in bed with the lights out and ready to fall asleep. The other period should be at your convenience during the day or early evening.

During the day, we recommend going into a room and closing the door, shutting out all distracting sounds. Lie down on a bed and relax as best you can for about five minutes. We know that after lying inertly for a time, the mind as well as the body tends to relax. We know that this passive state is the best possible one for conscious communication with the subconscious mind. After about five minutes, you mentally begin to give yourself those suggestions that you want for an additional five-minute period. You should use the pronoun "I" instead of "you." You not only mentally give yourself these suggestions, but you use the technique of visual imagery, imagining yourself concentrating and successfully accomplishing your goal. You should try to make this image as real as possible so that words and pictures will have a tendency to make an indelible impression upon your subconscious. We recognize the dynamic power of words and ideas. We further know that thoughts in themselves contain force. They have the dynamic power to stir, move, and charge those who are exposed to their influence. Our technique employs using self-directed suggestions for self-improvement.

As evidence of self-directed suggestions, you are probably aware of the inspiration that comes to geniuses in the arts during their periods of contemplation or day dreaming. The self-suggested goals which arose out of the inspired states of contemplation of such geniuses as Tschaikovsky, Beethoven, Dickens, Poe and Victor Hugo resulted in accomplishments that have the exceptional quality of universality. They could not have achieved these results by sheer will power. These results of self-suggestion and self-inspiration are interesting and enlightening and give further proof of the validity, practicality and efficaciousness of our technique for improving your powers of concentration.

The time just prior to actual sleep is the most important period for using self-suggestion coupled with visual imagery. For the rest of this chapter, we shall study this period and learn why it is such a potent one for influencing the subconscious. An analysis and discussion of this period in relationship to our technique will clarify your thinking as to why this period is so important to directing your thinking.

In the daytime period, you can give yourself suggestions during a state of relaxation. Just before sleep you are exposed to suggestions during a period of deeper and more complete relaxation and subsequently extremely suggestible. Suggestions given during this transitional period are especially helpful as they have a tendency to be carried over into the subconscious as the individual falls asleep. Here, then, is an important avenue to the subconscious. As you use visual imagery during this period, the impressions will spill over into the subconscious and be instrumental in instigating those attributes that you seek. The deliberate influencing of one's self through the use of mental pictures during a semi-sleep is not new. The priests of the ancient sleep temples in Egypt were first to recognize and utilize this period for physical and mental regeneration and inspiration.

Many of you can awaken yourself from sleep at a particular time without an alarm clock. Whether you realize it or not, you have used the technique of directing suggestions to the subconscious during the period just prior to sleep. The suggestions need not be spoken aloud. The mere thinking of the suggestions is adequate for our technique. For example, the thought of waking up at a certain time reaches the subconscious, and, because the subconscious never sleeps, it awakens you at the appropriate time. Many of us have gone to sleep with problems on our mind and to our surprise have found that we had worked them out unconsciously during the night through the use of the subconscious mind.

The subconscious mind controls us during the hours of slumber. We may roll to the edge of the bed without falling off because we are protected from doing so by the ever-vigilant subconscious mind. We also may become uncovered during the night and correct the condition without awakening because the subconscious registers the fact and tends to the matter automatically. You will recognize this procedure as another example of the subconscious acting as a servo-mechanism. Negative feedback (error-correcting feedback) was unconsciously sent to the subconscious with information that something was wrong. Automatically and involuntarily the subconscious made the necessary adjustments and caused certain responses to take place to correct and compensate for the body being cold. You should keep in mind that this is exactly what we are doing by feeding the subconscious a certain mental set that we want to possess. Any deviation from this set will be corrected automatically and result in continued, uninterrupted concentration. Obviously this psychological feedback involves a complex interaction between goals, motives and emotions.

Susceptibility to suggestion is present during the hours that we are awake. It is, however, modified and weakened or diverted by lack of attention and the interference of inept judgment. During a period of complete relaxation, when the subconscious is particularly susceptible to suggestion, distractions decrease while the imagination takes on greater strength. Impressions are accepted without question and are transformed into images and goals. There is no "static" on the circuit between the conscious and the subconscious.

The task before you is to make the best possible use of your imagination and suggestions. They are natural forces and instruments for gaining self-mastery. We have already stated that the prerequisite to using suggestion is the genuine desire to attain the goal you have set for yourself. It is this intensity of purpose that acts as the catalyst in the achievement of this goal.

It will quickly become apparent to you that suggestions coupled with enthusiasm constitute a tremendous force. We have already pointed out examples of this incredible power of suggestion and suggested that you can use your latent power if you are highly motivated. Habits of mind and body are created through constant repetition. Since the strength of our personalities is based on our attitudes and habits, it is important that we carefully condition ourselves for the best possible utilization of our concentration potentiality.

Let us go back to the period when you are in bed, relaxed and ready for sleep. After relaxing for about five minutes, you begin to use your imagination and start to see yourself concentrating exactly the way you would like to concentrate. Be specific and see yourself concentrating at a given task. If it's studying, conjure up an image of yourself absorbing, retaining and recalling whatever information you seek.

The use of the technique of visual imagery need not be confined to studying as concentration cannot be separated from most activities. Actually, you can visualize yourself being successful at anything. Suppose you have to give a speech, but always, in the past, had been very nervous before and during speeches. Every day during the two practice sessions, you could see yourself standing before the audience relaxed, at ease, and able to concentrate easily on what you had to say. This would tend to eliminate nervousness beforehand and help to insure a good speech. We have used this technique with very gratifying results in coping with the problem of stage fright in actors, musicians and vocalists. This same technique can be used with athletes to improve their performance. We have also used this technique with great success with numerous individuals who had difficulty in increasing their speed and accuracy in shorthand, speedwriting, stenotyping and typing. There is no limit to the application of the visual imagery technique.

Remember you are consciously instilling a positive success pattern in your subconscious mind. You must utilize the two ten-minute practice periods every day for success. The results you seek will not be accomplished by trying the technique for only a few days. Results will surely come to you, but you must practice the technique without reservations or doubts. Actually, the procedure must work. It would be impossible to use it without beneficial results. If you find yourself falling to sleep while giving yourself these constructive suggestions, do not struggle to be more alert. The suggestions will spill over into the subconscious until the moment you fall asleep. Do not let the simplicity of this technique cause you to doubt its effectiveness.

The questions most frequently asked in connection with the visual imagery technique are, "Will it really work in my case, and how long will it take before I can see results?" The answer to the first question is that it will work for you as well as it has for others. As to the time factor, it is impossible to answer precisely, as everyone presents a different problem. We have found, though, that once the individual begins to make progress, the program is accelerated tremendously because nothing succeeds like success. Most individuals employing the visual imagery technique begin to see tangible results in about two to four weeks. This certainly is a short period of time compared to the length of time the person has had the problem. We ask you not to prejudge the technique we have presented until such time that you have actually worked with it. We urge you not to formulate negative opinions as to the practicality of what we have discussed. It has worked admirably in too many cases to be shrugged off as not being scientific and efficacious. The authors stand ready to assist you if you need help. Chapter twelve will tell you about a free concentration service, and we hope you will take advantage of it should the occasion arise.

Psychology teaches us the art of creative thinking, but very few people ever do anything about it. It is possible to shake off the habits and shackles of the past and to create an entirely new life, based upon sound, proven psychological principles. These principles are embodied in the use of the visual imagery technique, coupled with other contributing factors that we have discussed.

Visualize what you want in your mind's eye. This mental picture of your life plan will work wonders for you. Most people idly think about wanting good powers of concentration, but that is the end of it. To actually achieve concentration, you must see yourself possessing this quality. Of course, you just can't dream about it. All great men were dreamers, but they translated their dreams into action. Goals must be visualized before they can be achieved and this applies to concentration. All programs of self-development begin with a mental plan. What you do with it is up to you. Your thoughts can be dissipated or they can be made to achieve the ends you desire. By visual imagery you can stimulate the creative powers that lie dormant within your subconscious mind. Visual imagery will enable you to channel your thoughts into a pattern of dynamic power which can be used for the purpose of constructive living.

William James said, "There is no more miserable human being than one in whom nothing is habitual but indecision." Once you have made up your mind to achieve better concentration, keep at it. You will achieve it if you persevere because the means will arise spontaneously. It is useless and unintelligent to try to achieve the impossible. Be realistic. Goals are important, but make them achievable and reasonable. Hitch your wagon to a star, but make it a star you have some possibility of reaching.

The acquisition of better powers of concentration is a reasonable goal that you should rightfully expect to achieve. We have presented the theories for acquiring this goal; the rest is up to you. You need only begin this very day, and you'll be on your way to a happier, more rewarding, more meaningful and successful life.

Chapter 6

Special Techniques for Better Concentration, Reading and Learning

No matter how proficient you become, concentration will never become so easy you can accomplish it haphazardly. Establishing a routine for concentration and learning is the most important aid you can utilize. Famous performers always follow a routine to make their work easier and they deviate from it as little as possible. This is particularly true of performers whose acts require timing and physical dexterity, but it is almost equally true of actors. Rehearsals are scheduled for the same time and place every day while actors are learning their lines. A large share of them also run over their lines just before going to sleep which corresponds to our suggestion that you can best accomplish visual imagery at this time.

A favorable mental set follows when you concentrate at the same time and place every day. In the first place, you will become so used to the furnishings of the room, the view from the window, and other physical factors that they will no longer distract you. As mentioned in a previous chapter, you will associate this room solely with study. The fact that you do it at the same time every day will prove of further help because the mind, with its built-in alarm clock, will automatically start thinking of study at the proper time.

Distractions such as radios and televisions, cluttered rooms, too comfortable chairs and traffic in the house and outside have already been mentioned, but they will bear repeating. Millions of people who have embarked on self-improvement courses are attempting to concentrate and learn in this type of environment. You cannot learn well and will soon lose interest unless these distractions are cut to a minimum.

Those who are taking self-improvement courses at local high schools or colleges can utilize many of the aids good students use in mastering their subjects. Two persons of exactly the same basic intelligence can operate at far different levels of achievement if their approach to learning varies.

The amount of time you study can make a great deal of difference. Even if you think you have learned a certain lesson in an hour, you will find it sinks into the mind much deeper if you devote another hour to going through it once more. A good rule of thumb is to devote two hours of study for every hour of class work. The authors, for example, are now taking a course in classical Spanish guitar. The class meets three hours each week and the authors have allotted six hours of practice. This breaks down to one hour per day, omitting the day the lesson is given.

Your study sessions actually begin in class with questions because if you do not ask enough questions to understand the assignment, you cannot learn it no matter how hard you try. Good students are never afraid to ask questions. They know they may fall behind permanently unless they understand everything that has gone before and what is required of them in the future.

Taking notes and underscoring important passages in study books is very helpful because the added activity helps to impress the facts in your mind. This is particularly important for those who are taking a lecture course but actually learn better through visual material. Ample notes should be taken in this case and they should be studied carefully so that the individual does not fall behind those who learn more easily through their sense of hearing.

Older people returning to study after years away from this sort of mental activity have a tendency to let old habit patterns dominate their attempts to study. Even though they have set a certain time to start studying, they seldom begin on time because they think of a phone call to make, a dubious need to drive to the store, something to be fixed around the house and a host of other time-consuming actions. Frequently these distractions take up so much time that study is postponed to a later time or another day. This type of procrastination should be recognized for what it is—a fear that the individual will not be able to concentrate or learn. The ultimate result is that the course of study is given up and lack of time is invariably given as the excuse. The inference to be made here is that nothing should interfere with the study routine. If you are honest, you will admit there are seldom real emergencies to interfere with your study.

In stressing the study periods, it is well to remember that you can study too long at one session as well as too little. There is a law of diminishing returns that sets in after you have studied so long you become restive. Vagrant thoughts and day dreaming finally overwhelm the mind and practically nothing is learned or retained when this mental condition has been reached.

When you have become restive studying one subject, it is not necessary to stop studying altogether. Take a short rest and then study something else. It is preferable that the new subject be completely dissimilar to the other one. Never try to study two similar subjects in successive sessions.

The amount of time you should study before taking a rest varies from person to person. In the first stages of learning how to concentrate, it is likely that thirty minutes will be as long as the mind can fix its attention before wandering. Later on, an hour or longer will not be too much. Remember, a short rest will always enable you to return to your work with renewed zest.

No book on concentration and learning would be complete without a discussion of methods to increase reading speed and comprehension. Poor readers and spellers seem to be the rule rather than the exception these days, and the question, "Why can't Johnny read?" has been asked by parents all over America. For several decades there has been a change in the method of teaching reading and it has become apparent that the change has not been for the better. Teachers in higher institutions of learning complain that their students read very slowly and do not comprehend what they do read. They blame the way students are taught to read at lower levels of education.

Whatever the cause, it is obvious that the more and faster you read, the more you will know because nearly everything we learn depends on reading. It is equally obvious the fastest reader in the world would gain no good from his reading if he failed to comprehend the meaning.

There are many causes of poor reading and any one of them may cause you to miss the message intended by the author. Concentration, of course, is necessary, but we will assume that you have made some progress in this direction in the earlier chapters of this book. A vocabulary sufficiently large to cope with the material being read is of major importance. If you continually encounter words with which you are unfamiliar, you will soon lose interest in the subject. Rather than go to the dictionary each time, you will abandon the project. This, of course, places a premium on developing an adequate vocabulary early in life. Those who come from families where extensive vocabularies are used have a great advantage. Those who do not must compensate by making lists of unfamiliar words encountered and learn their meaning.

A large vocabulary is the chief attribute of an intelligent man and such a vocabulary can be developed systematically by looking up new words every day. Once you have begun to delve into words, their origins and meanings, you will have embarked on one of the most fascinating subjects in the world. And you will have taken the first step toward becoming truly educated. The most important part of intelligence tests is that dealing with the knowledge of words. A large vocabulary and superior intelligence are presumed to go hand in hand.

It is not clear whether individuals read well because they have large vocabularies or whether fluency with words is obtained through reading. The authors believe the latter is more likely to be true, and particularly so if the reader will take the trouble to look up unfamiliar words as he goes along. The reader who attempts to guess the meaning of a word by its use in the context is apt to find he is missing the sense of much that is written.

Emotional and physical problems effectually prevent the mind from concentrating on the text, and those who attempt to read when under stress may read entire chapters without remembering anything. Such problems that become aggravated to the extent that it is impossible to fix the attention on anything require professional attention just as much as improper vision. Tests are now uncovering these problems in the young, but adults must discover their handicaps themselves.

One of the greatest lacks in our educational system occurs because young people are not told there are many different ways of reading. For example, memorizing mathematical formulas or historical dates requires different reading methods than those applied to philosophy or literature. Some books are written so that the reader may skim through very fast, absorbing only the highlights, and still gain sufficient comprehension. Rapid reading is not quite so superficial while detailed reading of technical material or learning a language requires complete attention to every word.

In deciding how a book is to be read, it is necessary to survey the purpose of the book and study its table of contents. Many times the jacket or foreword will give you clues as to how completely you wish to read the book. Most of us can remember our teachers often suggested reading certain chapters in an assigned book and skipping others. This was because it was felt that some chapters had no pertinent bearing on the subject to be learned.

The way in which you read a book should be determined entirely by what you wish to gain from its contents. Generally, you will want to read extensively in a narrative which depends on the unfolding of a plot. Such a book may be read rapidly but skimming may result in the missing of an important element in the unraveling of the plot.

Skimming is done when you wish to find the answer to a certain question, the name of a person or the incidents surrounding an event. Sometimes reading only one sentence on a page is enough to convince you that the answer you seek is not in that area. In this fashion the whole book can be skimmed until the exact information is found.

Reading is done at a slower pace when one wishes to form a critical judgment of the author's ideas. In such cases, the reader, through logical thought processes, must decide whether the ideas or theories are valid or invalid. Inasmuch as our conclusions are formed by comparing new ideas with our own experiential background, the reader must constantly compare what he knows about the subject with what the author is saying. When the material presented is completely new, the reader may have to compare the writings of several authors before he is able logically to accept or reject the material.

With the exception of elementary mathematics and similar subjects where only one answer is possible, it is suggested too that everything you read should be judged critically. Newspapers, magazines, books and advertisements all take stands that differ from each other and it is necessary to make an intelligent decision among them. Even textbooks have radically opposed opinions. The recent spate of books on the Civil War all point out various events as the most important in determining the outcome.

It becomes clear at this point that a great deal of reading must be done before one can arrive at a reasonably intelligent conclusion. Editorials in two different newspapers may be diametrically opposed on a certain civic issue, and a thorough perusal should be made before the reader throws his support to one or another.

There are many persons who, faced with the above situation, would wind up completely confused, not knowing which of the two plans merited their support. Such persons have never learned to grasp the salient points in written material which attempt to sway their opinions. They may read a great deal but without comprehension.

Reading with comprehension requires special techniques. If one is reading a novel, it is not necessary to remember every detail. The unfolding of the plot of a novel depends on a series of events and it is these events that must be remembered. If one keeps the sequence of events in order (take notes if necessary), it is easy to follow the progress of the plot. In concentrating on the events, the reader may find he also remembers many of the details because of their association with the main theme.

Sometimes details, although not necessary to the plot, add a great deal to the mood of the narrative and actually make the plot more effective. For example, the opening paragraph of *The Fall of the House of Usher* by Edgar Allan Poe actually states only that the narrator is on the way to visit his old friend, Roderick Usher. But the somber descriptive passages of his journey along the road set the mood for the horrible events that happen later. Constant practice will teach one to learn what is important and what is not.

In expository material, that is, material in which something is explained, each paragraph usually tells a fact which helps to develop the main theme. An excellent writer will invariably have his main idea in the first sentence and the rest of the paragraph will offer supporting evidence of his idea. Newspaper readers are familiar with this form of writing in which the main facts of the news can actually be grasped from the first paragraph or even the headline. Of course, a more thorough reading is necessary to get the background of the story.

The objective of all reading which has learning as its goal is thought stimulation. As you read, you must continually question yourself as to how the information being obtained may be fitted into your own plan of learning. Some readers accept without question the answers supplied by the writer and others try to organize them into a scheme that fits into their ideas or philosophy. This doesn't, of course, apply to concrete information such as dates or other data which are assumed to be true *a priori*.

Comprehension and speed in reading are linked closely together. For instance, if your comprehension is good, you will seldom have to go back to a previous sentence in order to understand the meaning of what you are reading. Poor readers must continually regress to earlier material and this slows them up considerably. In difficult reading, of course, even good readers may have to regress many times before they completely understand what they are reading.

Extremely fast readers have wide spans of recognition. This means that they are able to comprehend large portions of a sentence at one fixation of the eye. In other words, three, four, five or more words are comprehended before the eye shifts to the next group of words. In this way, ideas are grasped at a glance, the whole being interpreted instead of an individual word.

Individuals who speak each word to themselves or comprehend better by reading aloud need a great deal of practice in correct reading before they can keep up with those who read silently and comprehend words in groups. Persons who run their finger under the line being read or turn their head from side to side while reading also waste a great deal of time and usually lack comprehension.

Continual practice is the only way to eliminate bad reading practices and gain speed and comprehension. To begin increasing your speed, start with material that is easily understood and then interpret the ideas in sentences as quickly as possible. Instead of reading words, look for ideas.

When practicing reading, always read at a rate that is faster than your normal speed. Do not go back and re-read material while practicing. If you feel you have missed some of the meaning, re-read it through from the beginning for a second time. You will soon find you can comprehend all the ideas at the increased rate of speed.

Phenomenally fast readers utilize the technique of skimming. They may read one sentence in a paragraph or even as little as one sentence a page. They have learned the knack of looking for the cues which they have learned to identify as important to the total theme of the material being read. As stated before, this should only be done when some specific answer is sought, although the technique is used by many editors to determine whether a book should have a more thorough reading.

Despite the fact there are many formal reading courses utilizing machinery which forces the reader to read faster, the authors do not believe such measures are necessary except for those for whom reading continually is a necessity of their occupation. Reading machines expose the print at a certain rate of speed and cover up the material that has been read so that the student cannot regress. They work well but the motivated student can progress nearly as fast through his own efforts.

William S. Schaill, president of The Reading Laboratory, has devised a system he calls "phrase reading" which is as efficient as the most costly machine. Mr. Schaill recommends spreading a newspaper on a flat surface and then placing a card over a column of type. The reader then moves the card down to expose only the top line, glances at it and immediately covers the line again. The object is to see how much of the line the reader can take in at one eye fixation.

In the beginning, the reader will not be able to assimilate the entire line but practice will eventually result in a much wider span of recognition. Mr. Schaill suggests that the reader look just above and not directly along the line of type. It adds perspective and helps to learn phrase reading more easily. When you have learned to read an entire line of a newspaper column at one glance, you can move on to the wider columns of periodicals and books. Faithful practice will improve your speed and comprehension greatly.

The main thing to remember in increasing one's reading speed is not to force it to the point that comprehension suffers. After reading a piece of material at a rapid pace, see if you can write down the important points. Try this immediately after reading it and then an hour later. If you find you cannot remember most of the major points, you are reading too fast and must slow down until your ability to comprehend matches your speed. This, however, applies only to material you must learn for study purposes. Reading faster than you can comprehend is good for practice sessions because the comprehension will gradually catch up with the speed. Briefly, you force your mind to learn faster.

Whatever system you follow to increase your speed and comprehension of written material, it will be successful if you are motivated strongly and practice every day. Your self-esteem will be greatly enhanced when you find you are able to understand everything you read and this will result in reading more and more difficult material.

Chapter 7

Concentration and Group Learning

There are four broad learning classifications today and all of them have their separate problems and approaches. The largest class, of course, involves the millions of students who attend public and private educational institutions for the purpose of receiving diplomas, undergraduate degrees and graduate degrees which they feel are necessary to the careers they intend to pursue. Too often the purpose of teachers and pupils in this educational category is the accumulation of cognitive learning rather than cognition combined with growth in the pupil's personality and emotional maturity.

A second group brings together adults who are interested in learning special skills, hobbies or increasing their cultural quotient. A third group, numbering many more thousands every year, signs up for training courses which instruct them in the special qualities desired by their firms of employment for advancement. The last group is composed of those who study alone for a variety of reasons.

The first three study groups involve so many millions of individuals that it is necessary to study the many factors which affect concentration and learning in the teacher-learner relationship. It should be emphasized at the start that a learner is far more than an individual with an educational void to fill and a teacher's task involves far more than filling that void.

The real aim of education is to dynamically alter the student so that his internal thinking and external behavior are undergoing constant changes which affect his actions in life situations. The mere accumulation of knowledge which cannot be related to life situations becomes compartmentalized and its potential usefulness is partially nullified.

All learning which takes place in a classroom involves a complex interrelationship among the teacher, the individual and the individuals in the group. Learning in a group involves much more anxiety than learning in the privacy of one's home. Many more threatening situations arise, a self-image of adequacy is harder to perceive, and it is more difficult to rationalize failure when others are succeeding. These and many other factors become emotional blocks to learning that may result in defeat for a person whose intellectual capacity is probably entirely adequate in the situation.

A classroom situation is particularly threatening to an adult for several reasons. The very fact that he is an adult will make it difficult because he will find it distasteful to accept teaching from individuals who may be his junior in years. He will also have formed habit patterns of blocking out or distorting information which constitutes a threat to his self-image. He has been maintaining a semblance of ego strength by avoiding intellectual exercise, but he is afraid to test his ability in the "combat" conditions of the classroom.

Many adults will actually learn the material presented in classes, but whenever it threatens their self-image they will compartmentalize it. By doing this they are unable to put it to use in life situations. All of us have seen the person who has amassed a multitude of miscellaneous facts, but is unable to use them constructively in advancing himself.

The adult returning to the classroom after years of absence must be continually on guard not to use rationalizations and excuses for not applying all he learns. Many adults learning facts which disturb them do not actually forget them, but continue to live as though the facts were not true.

One of the authors is acquainted with a 30-year old man who decided to take a psychology course. One of the first facts he learned was that the intelligence quotient of Negroes was exactly the same as that for Caucasions. He considered himself free from prejudice but the fact was disturbing to his self-image. Although he memorized the knowledge, he was totally unable to apply it in life situations. He continued to think and act as if Negroes were below him in intellectual potential.

From a psychiatric standpoint, this man had a need to believe Negroes were inferior in mental acumen. His own feelings of inadequacy were so strong that it was necessary for him to believe this false theory. To paraphrase an old saying, if there had been no Negroes it would have been necessary for this man to invent them. He had to feel superior to somebody.

This is much the same position as is held by white supremacists in the South today. Many of them know intellectually that their innate intelligence is no greater than that of the Negro (or any other racial or ethnic group for that matter), but they are unable to accept the fact on an emotional level. They scream loudly about mongrelization of the white race to obscure the fact that the Negro, given equal opportunities, has already proved that he can compete in all areas in which the white man has been supreme.

Sometimes the inability of a nation to solve its problems leads it to finding a scapegoat to blame for all its ills. This is what happened when Hitler's inability to produce the results he had predicted went awry. With terror and violence, he spread the story that Germany's economic ills were caused by the Jews, who, he said, controlled all the money in Germany. This was in no way true, but it led to the greatest purge in history.

This leads us to the fact that we cannot like others unless we first are able to like ourselves. Treating others as you would like to be treated depends on how you feel about yourself. If your ego strength is low and your self-respect almost nonexistent, you are certain to feel cynical about the whole human race.

Once your own self-esteem has begun to blossom, you will find that you have more esteem for others. While you go about the task of improving your concentration and learning, it is a good idea to stop castigating and judging other people. Your own self-image, in some curious fashion, becomes more adequate when you cease to condemn others for their mistakes. To err is human and we are all human.

In all fields of learning, you will be continually exposed to facts that contradict what you have previously believed or professed to believe. You must learn to accept these facts even though they conflict with your self-image and many of the opinions you have held in the past.

Not all subjects, of course, are factual. Many desirable subjects in the humanities are open to interpretation by the individual even though they have been interpreted many times before. Literature and art may mean many different things to many different people, and you need not necessarily agree with the opinions of authors you are studying. The main quality you must have in studying the humanities is an open mind. Do not accept or reject any ideas or theories until you have thought about them at length.

Philosophy, particularly, is a field in which the serious student can learn the use of logic which will help him in forming a philosophy of his own. From Plato to Bertrand Russell, the field is filled with great writings of men who devoted their lives to evolving philosophies which try to explain all the mysteries of human existence. Their conclusions varied greatly and if you undertake to study them all, you will probably find ideas acceptable to you in all their writings. Likewise, you will find theories in all their writings that are unacceptable.

Reading the writings of the world's loftiest minds is not easy. It is pleasurable when your motivation and attitudes are correct, but it is never easy in the same sense that light novels or mystery thrillers are easy. You must bring strong concentrative powers to bear on every line or you may miss key messages necessary to understanding the main theme of the book.

It is in studying the humanities, those subjects not in the field of social or physical sciences, that motivation must be exceptionally high because there are no immediate economic rewards such as accrue to those taking specific courses to advance themselves in their positions. The humanities should be studied for the pure joy of learning and any economic advancement should be considered incidental. It is undoubtedly true, however, that the cultured person will inevitably rise higher than the uncultured one, not only socially but economically.

This brings us back to goals. It should be obvious that adults who decide to take a classroom course in any subject are dissatisfied in some areas of their lives, but not all of them decide to do something about it. Setting high goals is not realistic unless you decide to follow through by exposing yourself to the ego-testing situation of the classroom.

There is a far higher potential for learning in the classroom than there is in individual study, but there is also more danger that the learner may become discouraged and drop by the wayside. The latter is likely to happen when the group does not function as it should but is merely a collection of individuals in competition with each other.

The classroom reaches the epitome of its usefulness when each member feels a desire to help every other member so that the whole group goes forward at the same pace. The teacher of such a group is not continually beset with the problem of trying to bridge the learning gap between the head and the foot of the class. All members of a class where each feels a responsibility to the others are, in effect, teachers as well as learners.

The reasons for group loyalty by those who learn rapidly are not entirely unselfish. Classes tend to go at the pace of the slower members rather than the faster, and it is to the advantage of the fast learners to keep the slower ones abreast of the work. They will get more out of their classroom work than they would otherwise. It will be to your advantage to think in terms of group advancement as well as your own when you sign up for adult education classes.

Those who become discouraged in classroom work are invariably those who have failed in earlier classroom situations, that is, during their school days. Such students feel that their inadequacies will be publicly exposed, and the resulting anxiety is usually enough to prevent them from becoming successful in adult educational ventures. Statistics show that students pre-conditioned to failure may be inadequate in subjects even when they are highly motivated and interested.

It is absolutely essential that those who were not successful during their school days do everything possible to change their self-image. And it is particularly important if the class is the type in which individuals are pitted against each other. What little self-esteem and feelings of importance an individual has managed to preserve will be continually threatened in this atmosphere. There is little chance that he will be able to survive the feelings of insecurity and rejection which follow participating in such a class.

The authors are in close touch with many of the adult education classes at a local high school, and it is amazing to see the difference in results achieved by various teachers. Some classes start with more than 100 pupils and within several months are down to 14 or 15. Other classes lose no pupils as lessons progress from week to week. It is granted that the ego structure of some individuals is so weak they cannot stay long in any sort of situation where even a minimum of competition is present. But classes that lose three-quarters of their membership are obviously not being conducted in regard to giving consideration to all members. Outstanding members are singled out and concentrated on and the others gradually drop away.

You are not going to know, in many cases, just how the classes you join are going to be conducted, and this makes it imperative that you reinforce your own resources so that you will be able to complete a course *no matter how it is conducted*. With all the recent emphasis on education, there is still a great deal of difference in the ability of teachers, and you cannot count on getting one who is aware that teaching is a social process, an interaction of human personalities.

The thing to remember, however, is that the best teacher in the world cannot adequately support a weak self-image. It is up to you to strengthen your self-esteem to the point where you can stand the ordinary give and take of the classroom.

You will find your self-esteem and confidence are completely adequate for adult learning if you eradicate many of the myths about the situation. For instance, you must consciously avoid saying, "You can't teach an old dog new tricks" or variations of that erroneous adage. Test after test on adults at least 50 years old have shown that the chances are you will learn a great deal better as an adult than you did as a child.

Adults, in most cases, have much more powerful reasons for wanting to learn than children, and the advantage of this stimulus cannot be minimized. When you look in on an adult class and then compare it with a children's class you will easily see the difference in motivation. The adult class is still and concentrated; the children's class is plagued with distractions.

The fact that an adult has learned a little bit about many subjects is also of help. It has already been explained that a little knowledge about something creates the desire to learn more. Also, an adult, because of many life situations, is more readily able to relate new facts to previous experiences.

Another great advantage that adults have is that they will probably use their new learning in their daily life much more quickly than a child. Because of this it will become automatic quite quickly. A child usually finds no outlet for his knowledge for many years after he has learned it. In some cases he has to study it all over again by taking a refresher course.

Despite the fact that statistics are loaded in favor of the adult student, many fail because they cannot conquer the negative feelings about themselves that stem back to childhood when they received no praise or recognition. The techniques described in this book, if applied conscientiously, can help you change your self-image, but serious cases may need some psychological counseling. If you are unable to conquer persistent feelings of inferiority you should seek advice from a competent authority. Sometimes a visit to an adult class can help to lessen anxiety. The prospective student quickly finds out that the classroom situation is far different than he thought, and that he will be able to hold his own.

The biggest difference between children and adults in the field of learning is that the former come to school with no preconceived ideas or convictions. They are ready to absorb new information and theories because they have not lived long enough to develop counter opinions. Adults are very apt to be rigid in their thinking. You must constantly remind yourself that keeping an open mind is the infallible sign of youth.

Once you have signed up for an adult class, there are certain obligations that must be fulfilled—obligations to yourself and the class. If you have always been accustomed to keeping your own counsel, sitting quiet while others talked, you must learn to speak up. You must convince yourself that what you have to say is just as important as anything other members of the class will say.

Along this same line, you must learn to ask questions. Many adult students fail to ask questions because they feel it is proof positive that they do not understand the work.

This is the easiest way in the world to actually fall behind the rest of the class. Undoubtedly, you have been in situations where individuals whose knowledge you respected have asked the very questions you wanted to ask but lacked the courage. Questions pave the way to complete understanding.

When your self-image has finally become adequate and your self-esteem high, you will have no trouble in freely participating in classroom discussion. You will not be afraid to express an opinion even though it conflicts with the views expressed by the rest of the class. Of course, a dissenting opinion should not be expressed merely because you want to be different, but if you feel that truth is on your side you should defend your view with vigor. If further information indicates you are wrong, you should accede graciously.

With political propaganda and advertising blurbs surrounding us on all sides today, it is extremely important that you adopt a critical attitude toward everything you hear. Once you have developed a respect for your own reasoning powers, do not be afraid to reject anything that cannot be proved logically. Molders of public opinion gamble on your lack of self-confidence by making all sorts of assertions and claims that cannot stand analysis. If your self-image has really changed, you will be able to take a strong stand against such subterfuge, half-truths and downright lies.

It would be wrong to say that you can become a rugged individualist overnight. But persistent application to changing your self-image followed by whole-hearted participation in a class of adults can work magic with your personality in a very short time. All you need to start such a rehabilitation program is the desire.

Concentration and Group Learning

Although it is generally agreed that the classroom situation can lead to the greatest self-improvement, it can be a blind alley so far as personality development is concerned if all you seek is to duplicate and conform to others in the class. Despite the enormous pressures on the individual in this country to conform, it is usually non-conformity that produces anything of merit. Groups, by their very nature, exert strong influences on the individual to submerge himself and become a stereotype. There is a great deal of evidence to indicate that attempting to stamp out everybody in the same mold is not good for scholarship or the future of the nation.

Resisting the desire to attract no undue attention and "go along" with the group can negate the benefits which can accrue to those who are members of a group but still reserve the right to think for themselves. This age attaches tremendous importance to membership in strong groups, and psychologists are certain this feeling is traceable to the anxieties of modern man. He is afraid to be alone.

You will have to develop your sense of self-esteem to a high point to avoid the dangers inherent in the classroom situation. If it is high enough you will be able to listen to everything and still rely on your own judgment in the making of decisions. Developing an "organization man" should not be the chief aim of education. The chief aim should be the development of individuals who are not afraid to seek new ways and answers even though this process isolates them from their fellow students. There will still be a sense of "belonging" because the isolation will be intellectual, not emotional.

For the reasons given above, we are highly in favor of home study even though we recommend classroom work. Home study is more apt to produce original thinking, but until one has disciplined oneself to concentrating and learning every day, it is also more apt to produce procrastination, excuses and rationalizations. It is up to you to determine whether you can stick to a program of study alone, drawing all your own conclusions, or whether you need a classroom situation that requires regular effort but may stifle your originality.

Chapter 8

Communication and Semantics

Man differs from all other creatures in the world because of his ability to use words. They are the connecting links in all human relationships and the basis for all higher learning. The ability to communicate knowledge from one generation to the next by means of words accounts for man's unceasing progress in all the arts and sciences, and yet man is just beginning to use words for the highest purpose of all—universal peace.

More than anything else, the United Nations is a mass experiment in communication, an attempt to clarify through words the misunderstandings of nations which have heretofore led to war. And yet, paradoxically, without words there could be no organized warfare. The peoples of the world could not be stirred to hatred against each other because there would be no means of stirring up such hatred. There would be no mass means of communication to convey ideological differences, and the twisting of words to arouse anger would be impossible.

Newspapers, television, radio and other mass media daily tell us of man's monumental inability to communicate with his kind, and the result is world chaos. Unless man learns to raise his head above the sea of words by which he is surrounded, there is little chance that there will ever be world peace.

Because of the imperative need for man to use his unique verbal quality for good, there is a rapidly growing emphasis being placed on the fields of communication, semantics and cybernetics. Leaders in these fields labor constantly to improve methods and results of communication so that misunderstandings cannot occur at any level of society or in any culture.

Although modern transportation has decreased the size of the globe to a small fraction of its former dimensions, this shrinking has led to an increase of communication failure because the world's more-than-3,000 languages and dialects are still intact, and this language barrier must be coped with as never before. Any part of the world may now be reached in a few hours, but this new closeness has increased, not decreased, the problem of living in peace.

For many years linguists have advocated a universal language which all people would speak as well as their own, but this would be no assurance that people would interpret messages in the same way. This is proved by the fact that millions of people every day fail to understand messages directed to them in their own language.

A good example of this communication failure may be found in an old parlor game in which one member of a group whispers a sentence to the person next to him, and it is thus passed around the group. Almost invariably the sentence as understood by the last member of the group has no resemblance to the original one and though, in this case, the result is not important, this same thing happens in all types of communication.

Because of the increasing complexity of the world and the problems it engenders, the study of semantics and general semantics has grown greatly in the last few years. The International Society for General Semantics defines semantics as the systematic study of meaning while general semantics is considered the study and improvement of human evaluative processes with special emphasis on the relation to signs and symbols, including language.

The goals of general semantics are to help the individual, in an increasingly confused environment, to evaluate his world; to improve communication between individuals and also between groups of all sizes. The latter, of course, would include nations. The third is to use communication in curing mental illness, but this goal will not be of concern to us in this book. For those of you who would like to pursue this course of study further, we highly recommend the book, *People in Quandaries, The Semantics of Personal Adjustment* by Wendell Johnson, Ph.D. This book shows how the scientific method, including the scientist's efficient way of using language, which has revolutionized our physical world, can be applied to help us deal effectively with our personal and social problems—in home, school, and office, in government and industry, and in life situations generally. This stimulating and unusually practical book examines the relation of language to many aspects of human behavior in an interesting, fascinating and enlightening manner.

You will notice in the definition of general semantics that mention is made of signs and symbols as well as language. This is because of the fact that communication at a nonverbal level may sometimes be more informative than communication at the verbal level. Facial expressions, tone of voice, choice of words and the amount of talk determines what the listener perceives at the verbal level. Nonverbal communications such as shrugs, hand movements, facial expressions and silence itself many times convey attitudes and emotions more effectively than speech. Generally speaking, we might say that we convey thoughts verbally and feelings nonverbally.

The amount of learning you will be able to achieve in the classroom will depend entirely on how you interpret the words of the teacher. If you have great difficulty in determining the meaning of a teacher's message, you may be sure that your motivation is not as strong as it should be. As mentioned earlier, you can concentrate and learn much better when your motivation is high, and this is also true in perceiving the sense of a communication.

The reason our standard intelligence tests are mostly based on verbal abilities is because the amount a person talks about a subject usually indicates more knowledge. This as explained is not an invariable rule but it generally holds true. If you will recall your school classes, you will remember that those who talked the most, gave the most answers and generally participated more fully in discussions were those you thought of as superior, more confident, and more likely to be successful.

Communication in the classroom occurs at many levels and between many individuals besides the teacher. A class that has been together for some time develops a feeling of interdependence and reciprocal support, and many times the achieving group will go out of its way to help those who are not learning at the established rate. Conversely, the class will direct a great deal of its attention to those who have become leaders through their verbal ability in an attempt to identify with them.

Whether you are studying at home or in a classroom, the task is to make words work for you. To do this, you must not only learn the meaning of words out of context, that is, the dictionary definition, but also the meaning of words as they are used in relation to the whole body of the subject you are studying. Our language is so constructed that one word may have many meanings and it is important to know which meaning is applicable to what you are reading.

There are many reasons for communication failure. Chief among them, perhaps, is gobbledygook or the tendency to use a dozen words where one would suffice. There is an increasing tendency to do this in large organizations and in many specialized branches of the arts and sciences, and the individual must subject much of what he reads to intensive scrutiny to find out what is really being said. Failure to assemble all facts before arriving at a judgment also results in a lack of communication. In this way, people keep all their old prejudices and opinions without getting the facts.

The same thing happens when people use only two-valued instead of multi-valued logic. To this large group of people, a thing must be either black or white and no shades of grey are ever considered. This happens very frequently to those who accept the evaluations of our mass mediums of communication as true without subjecting them to logic or reason. Two-valued logic has no place in a world where cultures differ as radically as the languages.

One of the chief reasons communication may fail is because people fail to listen. Because of the vast sea of words around us all the time, some people conclude that nobody has anything worth saying, and consequently fail to listen or read in an effort to form new opinions. This is very common in the American culture.

If you are planning on any sort of work which involves communication with other nationalities and cultures, you must constantly school yourself to remember the differences in the backgrounds of your listeners. Many ludicrous and even tragic mistakes have been made by statesmen who interpreted what they heard in a foreign country in the light of their own background. There have been occasions when just such misinterpretation has led to war.

Another American characteristic which leads to improper communication is the habit of overgeneralization. Many people, notably politicians, establish one or two points which are true and hope they will override the critical impulses of listeners to investigate whether all the points they imply are equally true. All too often we have been conditioned by our mass media to guilt by association and our opinions are strongly influenced by statements carrying the weight of some influential figure or medium of communication even though the statements will not stand intelligent scrutiny.

Scholars for many centuries have used the syllogism to prove or disprove certain statements. The syllogism is composed of a major premise, a minor premise and a conclusion. Used correctly, it is a useful tool, but it can be perverted to serve special interests. All your powers of concentration, learning and experience should be used to check all conclusions that have been reached through syllogistic reasoning.

An example of arriving at an improper conclusion through syllogistic reasoning might be the following:

1. The American Medical Association is against any form of socialized medicine.

2. Dr. Jones is a member of the A.M.A.
3. Dr. Jones is against any form of socialized medicine.

In examining this syllogism, it is clear that Dr. Jones has been branded by association. Of course, it may be true that Dr. Jones is against any form of socialized medicine, but it cannot be stated with certainty. It is a matter of record that there are doctors in favor of some form of socialized medicine.

We have chosen this particular syllogism because it is so very nearly true. Other false conclusions are much more untrue, such as all Russians hate the United States or that the white race is superior to all others. Such conclusions are so common that you must use your concentration and learning to probe deeply into all of the things you have taken for granted. Learn to evaluate everything you hear and read.

One of the chief reasons for learning is to develop an open mind, one that can accept new concepts, but at the same time weigh them with care. Great scientists are distinguished by the flexibility of their minds. They are willing to investigate all new theories with a willingness to believe even if they eventually reject them.

It is this open mind you must bring to all your studies. Without it your concentration can be nullified because you are concentrating on the wrong things. This happens many times when a teacher or writer is trying to convey a message at one level and the pupil or reader is trying to receive it at a different one.

Good examples of this sort of communication breakdown exist today in modern art and poetry. The trail blazers in these arts are trying to communicate at a symbolic or abstract level while millions of persons are trying to view and read their works at the old reality level.

This brings out the fact that you cannot widen your horizons unless you are able to communicate and understand communications at many levels. The modern artist, for instance, may distort a man in order to bring out his emotional feeling about him. Those with closed minds merely say, "The artist must be crazy. That doesn't even look like a man." The artist, on the other hand, feels he might just as well take a picture if all he wishes to project is reality.

Remember this the next time you are tempted to dismiss certain study material with the old rationalization, "Why should I study this? What good will it ever do me?" Be honest and admit that you do not wish to study the material because it may prove too difficult. Actually, there is very little too difficult for the average person if he will work hard and try to perceive all communications at their proper level.

The teacher who asks why Dunkirk and Normandy were important is only incidentally interested in the dates, number of persons participating in these actions or even the number of casualties. What he is interested in is that the former constituted a turning point for the English people and the latter marked the turning point of World War II. If you know only facts and figures concerning certain things but do not know their deeper significance, you are only communicating at a superficial level.

Why is all this talk about communications so important? It is because man, for the first time in history, has the capacity to destroy himself. Communication has always been important, but never before has the fate of the world hung in the balance as nations attempt to interpret the meaning of millions of words flowing from other nations.

Diplomats struggle to couch their notes to other diplomats in language that will be firm but not arrogant, strong but not war-like, or friendly but not ingratiating. It is a tremendous task and the fact that these messages must be translated adds to the danger. A word in our language may have a different meaning in another, and even linguists are not able to keep up with subtle differences in meaning that could precipitate trouble.

Because the present state of world affairs makes translation an important problem in our crucial struggle for survival, linguists since 1948 have sought to use modern computers as a means of translating messages from one language to another. The goal, of course, is to develop a computer so accurate that misinterpretations would be impossible.

There have been many obstacles to the perfection of such a computer. It is easy enough to program enough information into a computer to make it an automatic dictionary capable of speeding up the process of finding language equivalents from one language to another, but as any student of a foreign language knows this is not enough. Finding word-for-word substitutions, even in similar languages, does not always produce grammatical or even intelligible translations.

A computer, to be successful, must have a set of instructions programmed into it which would enable it to correctly interpret ever changing idioms, rearrange words and decide among alternative translations. In addition it would have to know a great deal about grammar. Theoretically, there is no reason why this cannot be done, but in actuality it is extremely difficult.

Despite the increasing size and efficiency of computers, the human brain, with its 15 billion memory cells, is still vastly more complicated than the biggest computer ever built, and the average educated American still knows far more than could be encoded for use in a computer as big as a city block. The linguists hope this problem can be solved, but in the meantime we are going to have to depend on human beings to keep us from getting into communication and semantic difficulties.

In face-to-face meetings the danger of communication breakdown increases. Without the time to sit down and measure the impact of every word, there is more chance that world leaders will commit themselves to statements they had not intended. One ill-advised word can change a high level conference into a series of angry denunciations by representatives of all nations. It has happened many times.

You may say that all this is undoubtedly true, but it has nothing to do with you. You are wrong. Every day you are deluged with words that affect your opinion on matters of international, national, state and local concern. These words are written so that you will form an opinion without thinking. They are meant to influence you into believing whatever a special interest group wants you to believe. These words are the stuff of which propaganda is made.

It is up to you, as a citizen of what has become one world, to use logic and reason in determining your beliefs and disbeliefs. Your ability to understand and accept new ideas while discarding outworn myths and cliches will determine whether the world is to live in peace or destroy itself.

More than three centuries ago, John Donne said: "No man is an *Iland,* intire of it selfe; every man is a peece of the *Continent,* a part of the *maine;* if a *Clod* bee washed away by the *Sea, Europe* is the lesse, as well as if a *Promontorie* were, as well as if a *Mannor* of thy *friends* or of *thine owne* were; any mans *death* diminishes *me,* because I am involved in *Mankinde:* And therefore never send to know for whom the *bell* tolls; It tolls for *thee.*"

Ernest Hemingway republished those words in 1940 as a prelude to *For Whom the Bell Tolls.* They were meant to recall to individual men that they were a part of all mankind. They were fitting then and they are more fitting now.

It would be a good idea to study these words as one of your first lessons in perceiving a communication at the level at which it was written. If you do this, you will no longer wonder how you can affect mankind. You are mankind.

Chapter 9

Juvenile Delinquency, Crime and Learning

Sociologists, penologists and educators have long pointed out that there is a strong relationship between juvenile delinquency, adult crime, welfare scandals, youthful unemployment and low academic achievement. Many older inmates in penal institutions in the United States have not progressed beyond the eighth grade although this figure will be slightly raised in the future by compulsory school laws (usually until 16). Even so, it is obvious that criminals will continue to leave much to be desired from an educational standpoint.

Dr. James Conant of Harvard, who has done more than any other educator to acquaint America with its faulty educational system, particularly the secondary schools, declares the present situation is social dynamite and that the problem is growing. He declares that some 2.5 million of the 10.8 million students now in high school will quit to become an unemployable segment of the labor market. It does not require much imagination to see what will happen to many of these youths if they are unable to find work. And it is equally clear that many will not find work because the unemployment rate for those lacking high school diplomas is nearly double the rate for those with diplomas.

Even if a youth does not become a delinquent, it is not likely that he will become an integrated member of society. Many will end up on the welfare rolls because there is less and less demand for unskilled labor. Although professional and technical jobs are expected to increase by 40 percent in the next ten years, few of the high school drop-outs will be considered as candidates for these jobs. Neither will they be fitted for the 28 percent increase in clerical and sales positions nor the 22 percent rise in skilled labor. The picture is grim indeed.

Every effort is being made to keep these youths in school until graduation. Vocational training is being stepped up for those who show no aptitude for a liberal education, and individual counseling is being increased for those who quit school for scholastic rather than economic reasons. Work-study programs are also receiving more stress.

But this attempt to keep these students in school has its penalties also. Most of them—and they come to around 20 percent of the school population—are called "slow learners." Lacking in motivation to learn orthodox subjects, they are also the least able to absorb subjects that would make them skilled workers in technical fields. There is no question that encouraging them to stay in school acts to the detriment of students who are brighter in the conventional sense. They find themselves being retarded to the pace of their slower classmates.

The reaction of educators so far has been that these slow learners are incapable of being trained for skilled work. No doubt this is true of many who actually have basic intelligence deficiencies, but it is also true that the potentiality of many others could be salvaged by a comprehensive and enlightened program.

At the risk of repetition, we should like to state that many of these poor students come from environments that preclude any chance of success in school if educators continue to label them as inferior junior citizens. Somehow—in the school system—they must be allowed to become successful at something.

Initially, all children seek recognition. If it is not forthcoming at home, it is up to the school system to provide it. We are well aware that the anxieties and feelings of inadequacy that afflict children from poor environments make proper study almost an impossibility. But we are also aware that children who can find no recognition in school are very likely to seek recognition in a gang which derives its sense of belonging from antisocial behavior. It is axiomatic that juvenile gang members were poor students who became drop-outs, and promiscuous young girls and unwed young mothers almost always show a record of poor academic achievement.

Because millions of students drop out of school after the tenth grade, we believe it is necessary to take a fresh look at psychological factors that contribute to failure or success in students. We feel that many poor students embark on a career of crime to escape from the frightening element of scholastic competition, and that crime offers a hope of recognition even though it is bad. The latter point is proved by the many people who confess to crimes they never committed. Underlying their willingness to confess to crimes which may even lead to execution is the need for recognition although such recognition is not of a type most people would seek. Psychiatrists recognize that these people may have a need for punishment also because they feel they are "no good." Along this line, consider children who engage in mischief even when they know they will be reprimanded and punished.

We realize that no single approach will solve the problem of juvenile delinquency and crime traceable to an early failure pattern in the school system. But we submit that if the school system would give these students recognition in any field of endeavor, a great deal of crime, human suffering and expense would be avoided.

Undoubtedly, many students labeled as slow learners have congenitally low intelligence, but to stigmatize them all as deficient is surely an overstatement. Intelligence tests are being thought of as more and more unreliable by leading psychologists who point to remarkable records made by students in special classes whose intelligence was rated as low by the standard school tests. It has turned out many times that they only needed special attention and handling to develop latent talents that have surpassed those of their more conventionally "smart" schoolmates.

Most of these students who were given special opportunities to develop their "off beat" talents suffered from a great deal of hostility because of their inability to keep up with their classmates in learning conventional material. Their self-image was distorted and lowered to the point where their self-esteem was practically non-existent, and many of them had already become disciplinary problems.

A great many of these students started with a desire to learn, but lacking the verbal skills that usually distinguish the conventionally successful student, they soon fell behind. Their shame and hostility because of this resulted in their taking even less part in class discussion and they soon had a confirmed failure pattern. In special classes where they were allowed to seek out their special skills, they were given encouragement and recognition from the start. In case after case it was proved that these "hopeless" students were inferior only when no one took the trouble to uncover their area of superiority.

The complaint of all these students is that they cannot seem to concentrate on classroom material. Inasmuch as most students seem able to grasp the subjects, they soon feel left out of everything. "After all," they reason, "something must be wrong with me if I can't keep up with the rest of the class." Suicide is not unknown in such cases. At the very least, these students become psychic cripples and quite a few of them seek a sort of satisfaction in antisocial acts.

These antisocial acts are going to continue as long as we base our opinion of a student on the record he makes in the standard I. Q. tests. "The intelligence quotient tests," states Dr. Kenneth B. Clark, professor of psychology at New York's City College, "are worse than meaningless, they are seriously misleading. An I.Q. score is meaningful only under rigorously controlled conditions of individual testing by a trained psychologist who can draw out the best in a child and who can remain sensitive to the level of the child's motivation during testing."

It may come as a shock to many laymen to learn that I.Q. tests are heavily loaded in favor of the children of economically stable and well-educated parents. We have come to think of them as testing the child's innate ability, but they are much more likely to reflect the home environment because they rely heavily on vocabulary and other cultural factors which are dependent on books and conversations more likely to be present in well-to-do homes maintained by educated parents. Environment makes so much difference that it has been established that one out of four children scores above 125 in prosperous neighborhoods, the figure dropping to one out of 16 in poor neighborhoods.

Every day we condemn potentially gifted children to all the hazards of being cast adrift because teachers, intentionally or not, concentrate their attention on those students in the upper ten percent of the class who score high in the standard tests. At the very most they include those who may be called "average" but no attention is paid to those who score low.

It is the opinion of many psychologists that the mind is far too subtle and complex to be represented by a single score resulting from a few tests which are not really tests of innate ability at all, but, rather, point up the advantages of a favorable environment.

Standard tests, usually taking only about 30 minutes, test only vocabulary, number ability, memory, general reasoning, ability to visualize spatially and speed of perception. This may be all to the good, but such tests avoid rating the ability to reason beyond conventional methods and think of original solutions. All the emphasis is placed on giving a high score to conformists who do no creative thinking whatever. Actually, all but one of the areas in the standard tests were ranked below 20th in importance when a group of outstanding scientists were questioned.

In support of our theory, Dr. E. Paul Torrance of the University of Minnesota's Bureau of Educational Research has published the test results of several hundred school children using standard I. Q. tests and special tests designed to measure creativity. He reports, "No matter what measure of I. Q. is used, if we take the top 20 per cent of scores, we would exclude about 70 per cent of our most creative children."

It has been his experience that there is very little relation-ship between scoring high on standard I. Q. tests and the ability to be creative. "The nature of traditional intelligence tests," he says, "does not directly involve the ability to create new ideas or things."

Another important factor in standard I. Q. tests is speed. It would almost seem that the educators place a premium on superficial thinking and the ability to recognize a conventional right answer. The more profound and reflective thinker is penalized because he consumes more time in trying to arrive at a conclusion which has been the result of logical (but more time consuming) reasoning.

All of these things become pertinent to our chapter heading when we realize that the very ones who may possess the most latent ability and creativity are the ones being neglected by the school system. Many of them are the ones who will develop a sense of failure, inadequacy and not belonging merely because they are square pegs in round holes. Among them will be many who will drop out of school, become dependent on welfare, be unemployable because they lack a diploma and eventually turn to anti-social activity because they feel they have no place in the general order of things.

This thought is dismaying and the inescapable opinion is that we may be encouraging mediocrity and discouraging qualities we need more. One enlightened psychologist after another is joining the ranks of those who believe the stigmatizing I. Q. tests should be abandoned entirely and that each child should be tested separately in a large variety of areas.

The answer seems to lie in special handling for those who are now considered "problem students" and "slow learners," and it is sad to reflect that the reason we do not attempt to utilize this vast storehouse of talent is educational economics. With juvenile delinquency, adult crime and welfare programs costing billions every year, it would seem that special testing and programs would pay for themselves.

A projection of our present difficulties indicates the problem will grow worse before it gets better. Our population explosion will result in even more drop-outs in the next few years and it is not hard to see that a permanent subsidized and parasitical group in our society is not too far in the future. Given no special attention and lacking the conventional skills, these neglected people will spend a lifetime unemployed at the public expense.

Everything that has been said in this chapter thus far is calculated to bolster the confidence of those who had difficulty during their school days and now wish to do something about rectifying their educational difficulties. There is no reason to believe—with literally hundreds of subjects to choose from—that you cannot be completely successful in some area of intellectual endeavor.

Nearly all those who dropped out of school because of academic failure rather than economic necessity present the same picture when they finally decide they want further education and widened horizons. Despite their new-found motivation, they are fearful, lack self-confidence and feel they will be unable to concentrate well enough to make a success of their new venture.

Fortunately, adult education is far different from the stereotyped education they remember. They will be given ample opportunity to indulge in creative thinking and will not be subject to grades and the fear of flunking. Even where diplomas or degrees are at stake, a more liberal attitude will prevail. The older student will almost certainly find there is nothing wrong with his power to concentrate. His past failures have been the result of lack of interest in the course of study that stressed the qualities he lacked, and his ability to learn and concentrate will be facilitated when he finds he is encouraged for his own unique qualities.

The number of creative artists in America who were poor scholars in the American school system is legion. Indeed, many great writers such as Ernest Hemingway deliberately avoided too much formal education in order not to stifle their unorthodox approach to writing. This holds true in all fields where a certain amount of concrete information is not necessary. An engineer, for instance, must get his degree, but a Picasso will not need it. The great artist does not want to be hampered by restrictions which are always part of formal study. Many great achievements have resulted when persons have not been "educated" enough to know that what they were trying to do was "impossible."

It is a great shame that the millions of students who drop out of school to become statistics in criminal and welfare records are not given the opportunity to find something at which they can gain recognition. Special handling of preschool children with behavioral problems has proved that practically all children are amenable to some approach involving concentration and learning. Once they have found something that absorbs their interest, the behavioral problems are solved.

Experimental private schools have shown time and again that the child who is bored, easily succumbs to distractions and is a potential delinquent can be salvaged by scientific methods of uncovering his chief areas of interest. Once his self-esteem has been restored by successful ventures in unorthodox areas, he is very likely to develop the motivation to learn the subjects that are considered basic to American education.

Adults contemplating a return to classes must convince themselves that there is nothing wrong with their ability to concentrate and learn. They must, through constantly positive thoughts, become consciously aware that their talents are not non-existent but merely unexplored. A change in their self-image will result in a changed attitude toward learning.

Although a projection of the present figures on high school drop-outs, juvenile delinquency and adult crime indicates the problem will become worse, there is some hope that educational leaders will, despite tremendous initial costs, evolve a program to utilize the latent talents of the so-called slow learners. With proper techniques, a great many of them can become responsible and successful citizens.

It is agreed that a poor home environment will be the hardest handicap to overcome. Anxiety produced by broken homes, continual parental bickering and poverty are a great handicap to concentration. And in many cases, despite vast sociological programs, little is done to remedy the root evils of poor environment. Most welfare programs aim only at keeping their recipients at a minimal level of economic subsistence.

Juvenile delinquency will decrease only when every child, regardless of economic background, is given a chance to gain recognition in the eyes of his contemporaries. Those who have lacked this chance all their lives will find it available in the many forms of adult education in our nation. A changed self-image based on the facts we have set forth is a step in the right direction to put millions of persons on the high road to success.

Chapter 10

Tests and Examinations

Theoretically, the reader of this book has no need for this chapter. If you have mastered and are following the techniques set forth in earlier chapters, you will never need to fear an examination. You will have established regular study habits which you never break, and your interest and motivation are strong because you never lose sight of the end results—your goal.

You have, through constant practice, been able to see yourself as the successful person you wish to be and your self-esteem is adequate because you have conditioned yourself to this vision. You know you are doing as well as, or better than, anyone else and you don't need an examination to prove your worth.

Or do you?

Actually, a small number of advanced universities have done away with examinations, basing their decision on the fact that strongly motivated students need no extra prodding to keep them on their scholarly toes. Perhaps this works out well in some cases, but the fact remains that competition brings out the best in most of us and the knowledge that we must meet a certain standard usually forces us a bit beyond our ordinary capacity. We study difficult assignments harder if we are reasonably certain they are later to become part of a test that may mean success or failure.

There is a strong counter-movement today against the multitude of examinations that determine an individual's skills, aptitudes and potentials for everything from a job as postman to president of a large corporation. The authors are not in complete accord with the type of tests given because of their standardization, and because this non-individualistic method of testing is very likely to exclude some of our most talented persons. But we are convinced that — because we are all human — some form of testing must be done. For instance, it is certain that most of you who purchased this book determined to adhere rigidly to every suggestion that would help you to attain the higher status you sought, but it is equally certain that all of you, on occasion, have allowed beguiling diversions to distract you from this purpose. This is human nature, and it is a rare scholar, indeed, who would forego his fraternity dance to stay home and bone up on calculus.

Examinations of some sort are necessary because of this human tendency to put off what is labeled as work for what is known as pleasure. An examination, however, need not be the bugaboo that has plagued students for generations. There is, for instance, very little chance of your failing if you have kept up with the classroom work from day to day. But in this instance, too, the educators leave nothing to chance. Teachers have long noted that some students who glibly toss off answers in daily lessons, sometimes fail ignominiously at examination time. These students are the type who read superficially, scanning that which should be read carefully, and retain their information only a day or two and then forget it.

This brings us to an important rule to follow in preparing yourself for an examination. Read and reread material until it is indelibly impressed upon your memory. If you read a fact once and several days later are unable to remember it, you are the sort of student who must reread all he studies. In the more difficult courses, this includes all of us.

We remember the date, 1492, because it was so strongly impressed on us, so inextricably bound up with America, that it would be almost impossible to forget. You can, if your try, impress all material on your mind by surrounding it with dramatic events as you did in remembering the discovery of America. In the foregoing case, who can forget, "Columbus in 1492 sailed the ocean wide and blue"? This is not just a bit of doggerel. Many famous memory experts remember an extraordinary number of facts by utilizing similar techniques.

It was mentioned earlier that some persons learn more easily through hearing, while others learn better visually. Those taking lecture classes, particularly those who learn more easily by reading, should be extremely careful and copious in note-taking. There is one precaution, however. The lengthiest set of notes will be of no use if the shorthand method you use varies from day to day. All of us have probably experienced the feeling of amazement and bewilderment when confronted with lecture notes taken several days earlier in our own "do-it-yourself" shorthand. What was perfectly clear at the time has become nothing but meaningless gibberish. It is, therefore, a good idea to work out a systematic way of abbreviating lecture notes that will be as comprehensible a couple of days before examination as they were at the time they were taken.

Although we would never for an instant suspect our readers of seeking advance information about examinations to be given, we may as well tell you that the old habit of keeping past examinations around for future classes to study has disappeared. Inasmuch as the most important questions about a subject must always appear in examinations, regardless of the teacher or the year, these were of great help to students who were likely to fail. Today, in most institutions of learning, examination sheets are picked up at the end of the period and are not available for future classes.

Most teachers, unless they are unnecessarily sadistic, will always give you some idea of the scope of the examination to be given. This in itself is a great help because you can limit yourself to the actual material from which the questions will be drawn. Knowing the material, you can now read it again page by page, thinking in terms of the varying degrees of importance of the facts which you have gained through preliminary study. Some students are addicted to underlining those passages they believe are important.

The best way to remember important material is to write it out. If the margin of the book is wide enough, the important part of each paragraph can be written into the margin. The reason why this way is better should be quite obvious. You cannot write something down without absorbing some of the meaning. If the margins are not large enough, take a large sheet of paper and write the important passages one under another in the textbook as they occur. In this way, you will not only learn the material but will establish its order in your mind. This is particularly useful in history for the dates, battles, pacts and treaties that are the sum and substance of the material.

If you are an adult studying a trade or other technical course, preparing for a civil service appointment, or completing your high school or college education, you will find examinations far different than they used to be. Many examinations today bear down heavily on the multiple choice questions in which you select the right answer from a long list of possible answers, the essay type examination in which you write everything you know about the subject, and the objective examinations which are of the true-false type. You can actually raise your score by many points simply by knowing what to do in each of the type of examinations that are in vogue.

The right way to take an examination is to read it all through before you start. Pay no attention to the eager beavers who start writing immediately without knowing whether some questions will gain more points than others, and those you will find easy to answer and those that will take time. Most authorities advocate answering first those questions which will bring the highest score. We, however, believe that quickly answering all those questions that are easy is the best way to start. It not only means that you have already achieved a respectable score without undue effort, but your confidence will be higher for the remaining difficult questions. One of the reasons for reading the whole examination through before starting to write is that (and this often happens) you will think of the answer to the hard question while you are writing the answer to an easy one.

Your ability to file away information in the subconscious which you learned in the earlier chapters will stand you in good stead during examinations. In trying to think of a particular name, for instance, it may elude you momentarily, but other names and events associated with this name will come to mind instantly and the proper name will not be long in falling into place. Remember, the billions of neurons in your brain contain the memory of everything that you have ever learned, and it only needs the right "key" to unlock any information you have ever learned.

In the true-false and multiple-choice type of questions, your subconscious will be of great value. Even if your answers were pure guesswork, you will stand a 50-50 chance of being correct in many cases, but this average is increased considerably by the fact that you have studied the material previously, and even though you think you are guessing, your subconscious mind will automatically make the proper choice.

One type of student who panics others in the class is the one who sits down to an essay type examination and begins scribbling for dear life. He will cover page after page but unless he is especially gifted, he will not necessarily get the highest score. In the essay type examination, it is far better to devote some time to organizing your ideas and their importance in the subject under consideration. What you really do here is mentally visualize an outline with the most important fact at the top, the next most important fact indented five spaces further to the right, etc.

You can see examples of the essay type question in any good newspaper story. The writer will have his main theme in the first paragraph and all the other paragraphs will be in support of that theme. Those who start immediately to write, often turn in poorly organized and redundant examinations that would fool no teacher of any experience. Padding out examinations to compensate for a lack of knowledge is an old dodge in testing.

The conditioned reflex is the real answer to the problem of obtaining success in examinations. When Pavlov, the great Russian scientist, proved that dogs who had been conditioned to associate eating food to the ringing of a bell would salivate the same way every time the bell was rung, he proved that a certain stimulus will produce a predictable result every time. It is the same in education. Constant reading and rereading of any assignment is certain to produce an automatic result. The subject matter, in other words, is learned for life. Repeatedly reading your classroom material will guarantee results.

This is all very well, many students say, when the material is dramatic and interesting, but what about the material that is dull. It is our contention, as stated earlier, that no study material is really dull if the student will try to relate it to life situations and goals. What must always be borne in mind is the application of what one is studying to the end results that have been chosen.

Many students avoid the dullness of textbook explanations by frequent trips to the library where subjects such as history are covered fictionally in a more dramatic and interesting fashion. All the information is there but it is interwoven with exciting details that make the whole subject alive. Some conjecture and fabrication are used in these books, but the important facts are there also.

The library habit is important also in helping you to uncover little known facts which will make your examinations stand out from the others and impress your teachers with your interest in the subject. Doing only what is required will enable you to obtain satisfactory marks, but it is the extra effort that induces high grades. No matter what the subject, instructors are interested in those who progress beyond the minimum or required standards.

Adults who sign up for no formal classroom work and depend on increasing their knowledge at home face a more difficult task. Without the added spur of competition and examinations, they will find it more difficult to adhere to their self-improvement programs. More and more outside diversions are available all the time, and it will require rigid self-control to follow the programs they have set up. The biggest complaint of those in this category are that they cannot find time to study in an orderly fashion. Social affairs, meetings, care of children, and a host of other reasons are given for not following their prearranged programs. They lead busy lives and most of them contend that every minute of their day is full of important activities. Of course, this is true to some extent but a large number of the excuses are rationalizations to salve their feelings of guilt. No one is so busy he cannot find time to study. He may not be able to do it all at one time, but there are odds and ends of time all through the day when short periods of time can be devoted to study.

Paperback books are now being published in every field. They can be tucked handily in a pocket or purse and can be perused whenever there is a lull in the day's activities. The busiest executive, despite his protests to the contrary, has minutes and sometimes hours during the day when he can study these books. Only your own mental laziness can prevent you from gaining a new fund of information every day.

The matter of the examinations, testing what you have learned, can be solved by asking members of your family or friends to quiz you on the material you have studied. Most hard cover textbooks have review questions and tests at the end of each chapter, and you can test your own advancement, if necessary, without help from anyone. It should be unnecessary to state that cramming, although still widely practiced by many students, is not the best way to prepare for examinations. Even if you score high after several all-night sessions, replete with coffee and other stimulants, the information will soon be forgotten and the course eventually will be a total loss. Reviewing important aspects of a subject several days before an examination, however, is an excellent way to recall the questions that will be asked. This is known as over-learning and it is helpful in all abstruse and difficult subjects.

Regardless of the merit of examinations being given in all fields of endeavor these days, it appears that they are here to stay, and those who would advance in whatever field they are interested in will do well to familiarize themselves with the type of information that is sought by the various schools or industries giving them. Because thousands of them are being given, authorities know to the decimal point the mark that is considered necessary for success or failure. At the risk of repetition, we will say again that many good students are lost because all the tests are standardized rather than individualized, but the standardized tests are given because a number of attributes needed for orthodox students or workers are able to be graded quickly and consistently. They are fair in that all students take the same tests, but they are unfair to students with special talents whose capabilities are not being explored at present. It is to be hoped that in the future, individual tests will be given to all students so that their potential worth will be brought out and they will not become members of the large number of drop-outs who are becoming a social problem in the American economy.

The authors of this book hope that none of their readers will feel discouraged because they do not fit into the pattern of orthodox education which stresses too much the aptitudes of the man in the grey flannel suit. Degrees and diplomas, unless you are going to be a teacher, are not as important as taking the courses that enrich your life, and your self-image can be high even though you do not take the subjects required for success in stereotyped ways.

We are in favor of courses that will lead you to success in your chosen fields, but we are also in favor of courses that have no economic value whatever but allow you to read and understand all the subjects in the humanities that lead to a richer inner life.

Chapter 11

Questions and Answers

The authors, in an attempt to find out what questions would be most frequently asked about concentration and learning, distributed copies of this manuscript to individuals of various ages and occupations interested in developing better powers of concentration. Following are some of the questions that occurred most frequently:

Q: Is there a short cut to better concentration?

A: If you did not learn to concentrate in childhood as a result of parental guidance, it will require a great deal of hard work to acquire this quality as an adult. The visual imagery technique described in this book is considered the fastest way to learn concentration. Because it utilizes the subconscious mind and the conditioned reflex, concentration gained through this method will become automatic sooner than with any other yet evolved.

Q: What are the main factors in achieving good concentration?

A: Strange as it may seem, the first factor that is necessary before one may begin to improve one's concentration is a negative one—dissatisfaction. Unless you are dissatisfied with your present powers of concentration, you will never take steps to correct the deficiency. The other factors mentioned in this book, such as realistic goals, desires, motivation and others all depend on your being dissatisfied with your present status, whether it be cultural, economic or social. If only one factor could be named as the most important to achieving good concentration, it would have to be a realistic goal. People of average intelligence are limited only by goals that are unrealistic or not set high enough to allow them to achieve their potential.

Q: Because of my age, I feel I cannot concentrate and remember as well as younger persons. Is this true?

A: No. Adults, for instance, are able to memorize facts to be used in the near future much faster than children. Even though this may be due in part to higher motivation, it shows that the machinery for concentration and memory remains unimpaired well into the older years. Elderly adults, given the same intelligence tests they were given many years before, invariably score higher. There are scores of comparisons, now that adult education is becoming so common, to show that adults make better students than children. Age is relatively unimportant in learning. Unless a person is extremely old, actually suffering from the effects of senility, age should never be used as an excuse for not being able to concentrate or learn. Famous people, such as Winston Churchill, Herbert Hoover, Bertrand Russell, and Picasso, prove that the desire to continue learning, plus motivation, is all that is necessary to keep one productive in the late years.

Questions and Answers

Q: I am a high school student. I have no interest in certain subjects and dislike the instructors. What can I do?

A: This is a very common feeling among high school students. Many such students think that learning must always be pleasant and interesting or they will fail. It is true that some subjects are more pleasurable than others and some instructors are better than others, but the student who has set long-range goals for himself is likely to be successful no matter how difficult the subject or irritating the teacher. These students forge ahead because they see everything they do as the means to an end. There are certain cases, of course, where certain instructors are so incompetent that action should be taken. In such cases, you should seek advice from your school counselor and see if the problem cannot be resolved in a way that is mutually satisfactory to everybody.

Q: I live in a large household in a neighborhood where traffic is heavy and street noises are quite aggravating. Is it possible for me to concentrate under these circumstances?

A: Although our book stresses the importance of reducing distractions to a minimum, it is actually possible to concentrate under the most adverse circumstances. As one's interest increases in the subject being studied, background noises will become less and less noticeable. You have probably noticed that you hear nothing when you are immersed in an exciting mystery book, and this same faculty for straining out distractions can be carried into any field where one has studied long enough to develop a genuine interest.

Q: I get very upset before examinations and many times do not even answer questions that I am familiar with. Is there any way I can control these "examination jitters"?

A: As you probably know, many students, not to mention public speakers and lecturers, experience this sort of anxiety before taking an examination or making a speech. They usually express this condition by saying, "My mind went absolutely blank." To overcome this, we would suggest the technique of visual imagery explained in this book. In the period you set aside for practice, visualize yourself completely confident, composed, relaxed and completing the task in an easy manner.

Q: I have a strong desire to improve my knowledge about many subjects, but I seem unable to sit still for longer than five or ten minutes at a time. What can I do to overcome this?

A: Individuals who are making their first acquaintance with concentrated effort are recommended to spend thirty minutes of study and then relax and do something else before continuing. You are probably a particularly tense and anxious person, and you may have to build up your ability to sit quietly and concentrate a minute at a time. Certainly you can add several minutes each day to the time allotted for study the day before. In a short time, you will find that you can concentrate as long as the average person.

Q: I notice that your book states that listening to music while studying detracts from one's ability to concentrate. If this is so, why do so many industrial corporations play background music for their workers?

A: Doing a routine job which never varies and attempting to master a difficult problem are two different things. Franz E. Winkler, M.D., writing for THIS WEEK magazine (Sept. 17, 1961) in an article titled, "Beware of Background Music," states, "Even more critical is the habit of children to study with their radio or phonograph playing. They may never learn to focus their full attention on anything at all, to develop the power of concentration and the invaluable gift of a strong will.

"To repeat: *The mental, emotional and creative abilities of man may become seriously divided between work and diversions.* While he may become even more efficient in the routine tasks of turning out mass products, his ability to *create,* and to deal effectively with new and unusual problems is bound to suffer."

Q: How can I overcome the tendency to let my mind wander and daydream while trying to concentrate?

A: Daydreaming is a way of living your life in fantasy. When it is not carried too far and the fantasies are within the scope of your abilities, it can be extremely beneficial. However, when daydreaming occurs in the midst of a serious task, it usually means the individual is disinterested and is seeking to avoid the reality of the situation. If your daydreaming occurs while studying subjects which are necessary to your future success, you are not strongly enough motivated and must decide whether the goal you have chosen is a realistic one for you. All time spent in courses which are not directly compatible with one's goals is still important even though they may not be necessary parts of the goal itself. This, of course, brings us back to the idea of pleasure. It is not logical to expect that every effort one makes toward a long-range goal will necessarily be pleasurable. The desire for the goal must be so strong that it supersedes any feeling of displeasure toward any particular subject which is uninteresting to you.

Q: Isn't the presentation of the visual imagery technique and its application to concentration as explained in this book an oversimplification of a very complex psychodynamic process, and shouldn't the individual seeking such help obtain professional counsel?

A: The mind is a most complex mechanism, and scientists still know far too little about its working. But the techniques recommended in this book can be very helpful for the average person. Throughout the book we have stressed that all of the techniques involved are for the average person and are not meant for pathological or retarded persons. If you feel that your inability to concentrate and learn stems from organic or congenital problems, you should seek professional advice. This book is directed toward the average person who is experiencing the trouble most people have in concentrating their attention on subjects that are difficult to them.

Q: I have been using the techniques recommended in your book since receiving the manuscript (about one week), but have noticed no appreciable improvement as yet. Is it possible that I am not fitted for this type of learning?

A: We suggest you continue the recommended procedure for at least another three weeks. It usually takes several weeks before one learns to relax properly and a relaxed condition is absolutely necessary before suggestions are automatically noted and filed away by the subconscious mind. You may rest assured that new engrams are being formed that will eventually produce the results you seek.

Remember, we asked you to try this technique for a month before passing judgment.

Q: I can't seem to see a clear image of myself concentrating. How can I overcome this?

A: This is the biggest problem with individuals who have trouble visualizing anything. Some people, women particularly, are able to visualize easily while others see nothing when asked to visualize. We are not all Walter Mittys, but we all have the ability to see ourselves in certain situations if we try frequently and conscientiously. If you cannot, at first, actually see yourself performing difficult feats, try to concentrate on the feeling that you would have if your wishes came true. If you are able to capture the feeling you would have if you could learn and concentrate without effort, you will eventually see yourself in the same role.

Q: What is the difference between visual imagery and positive thinking?

A: The two terms may seem to be synonymous but careful scrutiny will prove otherwise. Positive thinking deals only with the conscious mind. This is just the first step in using visual imagery. The second step is to indelibly record these positive thoughts into the subconscious mind while the organism is in a highly suggestible state.

Q: Isn't visual imagery, depending as it does on powerful suggestions, actually a form of self-hypnosis?

A: This is a moot question. It is true that hypnosis depends on suggestion and no one really knows where suggestion ends and hypnosis begins. But our visual imagery technique involves none of the dramatic phenomena induced by hypnosis. Both the authors have taught concentration and learning through the use of hypnosis and can assure you that the techniques involved are very much different although there is a superficial relationship.

Q: I cannot seem to determine whether your technique is working for me or not. At times my ability to concentrate and learn seems improved, and at other times it seems to be the same as it was before using visual imagery. How can I make my improvement permanent?

A: The periods of improvement in your concentration are proof positive that you can make the change permanent. The experience of improvement should be fed back into your subconscious and will be the beginning of a chain reaction. Our self-image changes and our self-confidence increases as successful ventures are filed away in the subconscious. Eventually these successes will outnumber the negative results and you will think and act in a successful way without conscious effort. Your experience is a sure sign that the conditioning process is working.

Q: I talked to some friends about using visual imagery for improving my powers of concentration. They didn't seem to think it was practical. Are there any outstanding people who have improved their concentration by this method?

A: Dr. Maxwell Maltz, a famous plastic surgeon, lists hosts of prominent people who have improved themselves through the technique of visual imagery. His book, *Psycho-Cybernetics,* has helped thousands through the application of this new science. Your authors highly recommend this book should there be need for further clarification of the visual imagery technique.

Q: I am not completely convinced that the visual imagery technique will work for me. Will this handicap me in obtaining results?

A: Any method of self-improvement will work better if the individual is convinced of its worth. This has been proved many times by physicians who often obtain just as good results from a placebo (dummy pill) as they do from a bona fide drug. Conviction of cure often leads to cure. In the case of visual imagery, we have no hesitancy in stating that it will be of benefit to you even if you follow the recommendations mechanically. Naturally, it will work even better when you are convinced it can change your life as it has changed the lives of so many others.

Q: I noticed in the book that some writer said he could usually start his ideas flowing by lighting a cigarette. Is there any data to indicate that smoking is conducive to thinking?

A: No. All the evidence is to the contrary. One of your authors has always smoked while writing and so believes that it has something to do with his ability to overcome "blocks" in his thinking. Test after test shows that smoking actually retards intellectual processes, and its devastating physical results have been pointed out in many medical papers. Incidentally, if you are a smoker and would like to give it up permanently we recommend that you read *How You Can Stop Smoking Permanently* by Ernest Caldwell (Wilshire Book Co.).

Q: I learned from your book that studying in overstuffed chairs or reclining couches is detrimental to concentration. I do all my studying in a reclining chair and have always maintained high grades and have an excellent mem-

ory for all that I have learned. Aren't there exceptions to this rule?

A: Naturally, there are exceptions to all rules, but it has been our observation that those who recline to study usually wind up by taking a nap. It must be borne in mind also that much studying requires the use of a desk so that written material can be prepared and a reclining chair would hardly fit into this picture. There is an old saying, however, that one should never tamper with success and if you are able to concentrate for an hour or longer in a reclining position, more power to you.

Q: Are there any activities outside of studying in which one can develop one's concentration powers?

A: There are many pleasurable ways of developing concentration aside from studying. Chess, checkers and bridge are excellent examples of games that provide pleasure while sharpening the powers of concentration. Any game that requires the player to remember everything that transpires helps to improve one's concentration.

Q: Is it true that computers will eventually take over all thinking processes now common to man?

A: No. A computer is a machine and can never do more than a human mind instructs it to do. Given the proper information, a computer can far outstrip man in speed of problem solving, but it would be nothing more than a mute mass of metal without man's guidance. A computer will never be able to think creatively without programming by man.

Q: My little boy uses far more words than are in his second-grade reader. Why do these readers use so few words when children are able to understand so many words?

A: The feeling in the past was that children, although they understood many words, could not be taught to recognize them in a book in the early grades. Because of this idea, children employing thousands of words were reading books which endlessly repeated from 200 to 300 words. Educators now realize that children are able to learn much more than is required, and a thorough revision of textbooks is in progress at the present time.

Q: I have heard there is a record that relaxes you and then programs constructive suggestions into the subconscious mind for better concentration. Is there such a record and can it be effective?

A: Yes, the authors of this book have made such a record, and it can be extremely effective in helping you develop your concentration, memory and learning ability. The record was made at the request of many persons who read the first edition of this book and wished to have the most important psychological techniques and special tips on concentration made available for listening.

As you know, some individuals learn more readily by reading educational material, and others learn better if they hear it. This is one of the reasons universities supplement textbooks with lectures, and it is the basis of the new audio-visual techniques now being used at all levels of education, in industry and the armed forces.

No matter which way is the easier for you, however, you will find the record invaluable in programming suggestions into your subconscious when it is most receptive. After you have become relaxed by following the suggestions in the first part of the record, you will find that you are memorizing all the other suggestions with little or no effort on your part. Within a short time your reaction to concentration and learning situations will be automatic — proof that the subconscious has stored away all that it has heard and has made it available for instant use without the necessity of conscious thought.

What this record really does is to help you attain the automatically correct results of an electronic computer. Your subconscious mind, having been programmed to react automatically to intellectual stimuli, furnishes the correct response pattern whenever such stimuli are encountered. It is essentially the same method used by mathematicians, scientists and problem solvers in general. Additionally, you will find you are acting on the suggestions calculated to change your feelings about yourself. Your self-image will become dynamically confident and you will develop the self-esteem necessary to solve your problems.

The record is called PROGRAMMING FOR BETTER CONCENTRATION and is available at $7.00 postpaid. It can be obtained directly from Melvin Powers, 12015 Sherman Road, North Hollywood, California 91605.

Chapter 12

Your Free Concentration Service

You have read of the importance of visual imagery combined with motivation and desirable goals in activating your subconscious mind for better powers of concentration. We hope that you will be able to implement the theories presented in this book for constructive purposes. There is no reason why you cannot emulate the successful results of the many thousands who have used this technique to improve their position socially, culturally and economically. It is important to reiterate that repetition is the key in using our techniques for better concentration. Develop unbounded enthusiasm for intellectual achievement and convince yourself that visual imagery is the best and easiest way to achieve it. The constant repetition of the visual imagery technique eventually causes an automatic response in the subconscious mind when matters requiring concentration and learning are presented.

If you have already tried this technique without apparent benefit, do not give up. Some people do not visualize as easily as others, and they will inevitably take a longer time to master the technique. If you have devoted what you consider a long enough time to have achieved results and still find no improvement in your powers of concentration, you are invited to write the authors of this book and enlist their help. There is no charge for this service and your letter will be answered promptly.

It is possible that you may still have questions about the visual imagery technique, even though your powers of concentration are improving. You may feel that you will improve even faster by further clarification of the principles involved. It is impossible for the authors to anticipate all of the questions that may occur as the reader practices this new technique.

Should you have any questions, doubts, misunderstandings or difficulties concerning the techniques advocated in this book, we invite you to write and send a self-addressed stamped envelope to:

Concentration Service
Wilshire Book Company
12015 Sherman Road
No. Hollywood, California 91605

ELVIN POWERS SELF-IMPROVEMENT LIBRARY

ASTROLOGY
_ ASTROLOGY: HOW TO CHART YOUR HOROSCOPE *Max Heindel*	5.00
_ ASTROLOGY AND SEXUAL ANALYSIS *Morris C. Goodman*	5.00
_ ASTROLOGY MADE EASY *Astarte*	3.00
_ ASTROLOGY MADE PRACTICAL *Alexandra Kayhle*	3.00
_ ASTROLOGY, ROMANCE, YOU AND THE STARS *Anthony Norvell*	5.00
_ MY WORLD OF ASTROLOGY *Sydney Omarr*	7.00
_ THOUGHT DIAL *Sydney Omarr*	4.00
_ WHAT THE STARS REVEAL ABOUT THE MEN IN YOUR LIFE *Thelma White*	3.00

BRIDGE
_ BRIDGE BIDDING MADE EASY *Edwin B. Kantar*	10.00
_ BRIDGE CONVENTIONS *Edwin B. Kantar*	7.00
_ BRIDGE HUMOR *Edwin B. Kantar*	5.00
_ COMPETITIVE BIDDING IN MODERN BRIDGE *Edgar Kaplan*	7.00
_ DEFENSIVE BRIDGE PLAY COMPLETE *Edwin B. Kantar*	15.00
_ GAMESMAN BRIDGE—Play Better with Kantar *Edwin B. Kantar*	5.00
_ HOW TO IMPROVE YOUR BRIDGE *Alfred Sheinwold*	5.00
_ IMPROVING YOUR BIDDING SKILLS *Edwin B. Kantar*	4.00
_ INTRODUCTION TO DECLARER'S PLAY *Edwin B. Kantar*	5.00
_ INTRODUCTION TO DEFENDER'S PLAY *Edwin B. Kantar*	5.00
_ KANTAR FOR THE DEFENSE *Edwin B. Kantar*	7.00
_ KANTAR FOR THE DEFENSE VOLUME 2 *Edwin B. Kantar*	7.00
_ SHORT CUT TO WINNING BRIDGE *Alfred Sheinwold*	3.00
_ TEST YOUR BRIDGE PLAY *Edwin B. Kantar*	5.00
_ VOLUME 2—TEST YOUR BRIDGE PLAY *Edwin B. Kantar*	5.00
_ WINNING DECLARER PLAY *Dorothy Hayden Truscott*	5.00

BUSINESS, STUDY & REFERENCE
_ CONVERSATION MADE EASY *Elliot Russell*	4.00
_ EXAM SECRET *Dennis B. Jackson*	3.00
_ FIX-IT BOOK *Arthur Symons*	2.00
_ HOW TO DEVELOP A BETTER SPEAKING VOICE *M. Hellier*	4.00
_ HOW TO SELF-PUBLISH YOUR BOOK & MAKE IT A BEST SELLER *Melvin Powers*	10.00
_ INCREASE YOUR LEARNING POWER *Geoffrey A. Dudley*	3.00
_ PRACTICAL GUIDE TO BETTER CONCENTRATION *Melvin Powers*	3.00
_ PRACTICAL GUIDE TO PUBLIC SPEAKING *Maurice Forley*	5.00
_ 7 DAYS TO FASTER READING *William S. Schaill*	5.00
_ SONGWRITERS' RHYMING DICTIONARY *Jane Shaw Whitfield*	7.00
_ SPELLING MADE EASY *Lester D. Basch & Dr. Milton Finkelstein*	3.00
_ STUDENT'S GUIDE TO BETTER GRADES *J. A. Rickard*	3.00
_ TEST YOURSELF—Find Your Hidden Talent *Jack Shafer*	3.00
_ YOUR WILL & WHAT TO DO ABOUT IT *Attorney Samuel G. Kling*	5.00

CALLIGRAPHY
_ ADVANCED CALLIGRAPHY *Katherine Jeffares*	7.00
_ CALLIGRAPHER'S REFERENCE BOOK *Anne Leptich & Jacque Evans*	7.00
_ CALLIGRAPHY—The Art of Beautiful Writing *Katherine Jeffares*	7.00
_ CALLIGRAPHY FOR FUN & PROFIT *Anne Leptich & Jacque Evans*	7.00
_ CALLIGRAPHY MADE EASY *Tina Serafini*	7.00

CHESS & CHECKERS
_ BEGINNER'S GUIDE TO WINNING CHESS *Fred Reinfeld*	5.00
_ CHESS IN TEN EASY LESSONS *Larry Evans*	5.00
_ CHESS MADE EASY *Milton L. Hanauer*	3.00
_ CHESS PROBLEMS FOR BEGINNERS *edited by Fred Reinfeld*	5.00
_ CHESS SECRETS REVEALED *Fred Reinfeld*	2.00
_ CHESS TACTICS FOR BEGINNERS *edited by Fred Reinfeld*	5.00
_ CHESS THEORY & PRACTICE *Morry & Mitchell*	2.00
_ HOW TO WIN AT CHECKERS *Fred Reinfeld*	3.00
_ 1001 BRILLIANT WAYS TO CHECKMATE *Fred Reinfeld*	5.00

_ HOW YOU CAN BEAT THE RACES *Jack Kavanagh*	5.00
_ MAKING MONEY AT THE RACES *David Barr*	5.00
_ PAYDAY AT THE RACES *Les Conklin*	5.00
_ SMART HANDICAPPING MADE EASY *William Bauman*	5.00
_ SUCCESS AT THE HARNESS RACES *Barry Meadow*	5.00
_ WINNING AT THE HARNESS RACES—An Expert's Guide *Nick Cammarano*	5.00

HUMOR

_ HOW TO FLATTEN YOUR TUSH *Coach Marge Reardon*	2.00
_ HOW TO MAKE LOVE TO YOURSELF *Ron Stevens & Joy Grdnic*	3.00
_ JOKE TELLER'S HANDBOOK *Bob Orben*	5.00
_ JOKES FOR ALL OCCASIONS *Al Schock*	5.00
_ 2000 NEW LAUGHS FOR SPEAKERS *Bob Orben*	5.00
_ 2,500 JOKES TO START 'EM LAUGHING *Bob Orben*	5.00

HYPNOTISM

_ ADVANCED TECHNIQUES OF HYPNOSIS *Melvin Powers*	3.00
_ BRAINWASHING AND THE CULTS *Paul A. Verdier, Ph.D.*	3.00
_ CHILDBIRTH WITH HYPNOSIS *William S. Kroger, M.D.*	5.00
_ HOW TO SOLVE Your Sex Problems with Self-Hypnosis *Frank S. Caprio, M.D.*	5.00
_ HOW TO STOP SMOKING THRU SELF-HYPNOSIS *Leslie M. LeCron*	3.00
_ HOW TO USE AUTO-SUGGESTION EFFECTIVELY *John Duckworth*	3.00
_ HOW YOU CAN BOWL BETTER USING SELF-HYPNOSIS *Jack Heise*	4.00
_ HOW YOU CAN PLAY BETTER GOLF USING SELF-HYPNOSIS *Jack Heise*	3.00
_ HYPNOSIS AND SELF-HYPNOSIS *Bernard Hollander, M.D.*	5.00
_ HYPNOTISM *(Originally published in 1893) Carl Sextus*	5.00
_ HYPNOTISM & PSYCHIC PHENOMENA *Simeon Edmunds*	4.00
_ HYPNOTISM MADE EASY *Dr. Ralph Winn*	3.00
_ HYPNOTISM MADE PRACTICAL *Louis Orton*	5.00
_ HYPNOTISM REVEALED *Melvin Powers*	3.00
_ HYPNOTISM TODAY *Leslie LeCron and Jean Bordeaux, Ph.D.*	5.00
_ MODERN HYPNOSIS *Lesley Kuhn & Salvatore Russo, Ph.D.*	5.00
_ NEW CONCEPTS OF HYPNOSIS *Bernard C. Gindes, M.D.*	7.00
_ NEW SELF-HYPNOSIS *Paul Adams*	7.00
_ POST-HYPNOTIC INSTRUCTIONS—Suggestions for Therapy *Arnold Furst*	5.00
_ PRACTICAL GUIDE TO SELF-HYPNOSIS *Melvin Powers*	3.00
_ PRACTICAL HYPNOTISM *Philip Magonet, M.D.*	3.00
_ SECRETS OF HYPNOTISM *S. J. Van Pelt, M.D.*	5.00
_ SELF-HYPNOSIS A Conditioned-Response Technique *Laurence Sparks*	7.00
_ SELF-HYPNOSIS Its Theory, Technique & Application *Melvin Powers*	3.00
_ THERAPY THROUGH HYPNOSIS *edited by Raphael H. Rhodes*	5.00

JUDAICA

_ SERVICE OF THE HEART *Evelyn Garfiel, Ph.D.*	7.00
_ STORY OF ISRAEL IN COINS *Jean & Maurice Gould*	2.00
_ STORY OF ISRAEL IN STAMPS *Maxim & Gabriel Shamir*	1.00
_ TONGUE OF THE PROPHETS *Robert St. John*	7.00

JUST FOR WOMEN

_ COSMOPOLITAN'S GUIDE TO MARVELOUS MEN Fwd. by *Helen Gurley Brown*	3.00
_ COSMOPOLITAN'S HANG-UP HANDBOOK Foreword by *Helen Gurley Brown*	4.00
_ COSMOPOLITAN'S LOVE BOOK—A Guide to Ecstasy in Bed	7.00
_ COSMOPOLITAN'S NEW ETIQUETTE GUIDE Fwd. by *Helen Gurley Brown*	4.00
_ I AM A COMPLEAT WOMAN *Doris Hagopian & Karen O'Connor Sweeney*	3.00
_ JUST FOR WOMEN—A Guide to the Female Body *Richard E. Sand, M.D.*	5.00
_ NEW APPROACHES TO SEX IN MARRIAGE *John E. Eichenlaub, M.D.*	3.00
_ SEXUALLY ADEQUATE FEMALE *Frank S. Caprio, M.D.*	3.00
_ SEXUALLY FULFILLED WOMAN *Dr. Rachel Copelan*	5.00
_ YOUR FIRST YEAR OF MARRIAGE *Dr. Tom McGinnis*	3.00

MARRIAGE, SEX & PARENTHOOD

_ ABILITY TO LOVE *Dr. Allan Fromme*	7.00
_ GUIDE TO SUCCESSFUL MARRIAGE *Drs. Albert Ellis & Robert Harper*	5.00
_ HOW TO RAISE AN EMOTIONALLY HEALTHY, HAPPY CHILD *A. Ellis*	5.00

_ MAGIC OF THINKING SUCCESS *Dr. David J. Schwartz*	7.00
_ MAGIC POWER OF YOUR MIND *Walter M. Germain*	7.00
_ MENTAL POWER THROUGH SLEEP SUGGESTION *Melvin Powers*	3.00
_ NEVER UNDERESTIMATE THE SELLING POWER OF A WOMAN *Dottie Walters*	7.00
_ NEW GUIDE TO RATIONAL LIVING *Albert Ellis, Ph.D. & R. Harper, Ph.D.*	3.00
_ PROJECT YOU *A Manual of Rational Assertiveness Training Paris & Casey*	6.00
_ PSYCHO-CYBERNETICS *Maxwell Maltz, M.D.*	5.00
_ PSYCHOLOGY OF HANDWRITING *Nadya Olyanova*	7.00
_ SALES CYBERNETICS *Brian Adams*	7.00
_ SCIENCE OF MIND IN DAILY LIVING *Dr. Donald Curtis*	5.00
_ SECRET OF SECRETS *U. S. Andersen*	7.00
_ SECRET POWER OF THE PYRAMIDS *U. S. Andersen*	7.00
_ SELF-THERAPY FOR THE STUTTERER *Malcolm Frazer*	3.00
_ SUCCESS-CYBERNETICS *U. S. Andersen*	6.00
_ 10 DAYS TO A GREAT NEW LIFE *William E. Edwards*	3.00
_ THINK AND GROW RICH *Napoleon Hill*	5.00
_ THINK YOUR WAY TO SUCCESS *Dr. Lew Losoncy*	5.00
_ THREE MAGIC WORDS *U. S. Andersen*	7.00
_ TREASURY OF COMFORT *edited by Rabbi Sidney Greenberg*	5.00
_ TREASURY OF THE ART OF LIVING *Sidney S. Greenberg*	5.00
_ WHAT YOUR HANDWRITING REVEALS *Albert E. Hughes*	3.00
_ YOU ARE NOT THE TARGET *Laura Huxley*	5.00
_ YOUR SUBCONSCIOUS POWER *Charles M. Simmons*	7.00
_ YOUR THOUGHTS CAN CHANGE YOUR LIFE *Dr. Donald Curtis*	7.00

SPORTS

_ BICYCLING FOR FUN AND GOOD HEALTH *Kenneth E. Luther*	2.00
_ BILLIARDS—Pocket • Carom • Three Cushion *Clive Cottingham, Jr.*	5.00
_ CAMPING-OUT 101 Ideas & Activities *Bruno Knobel*	2.00
_ COMPLETE GUIDE TO FISHING *Vlad Evanoff*	2.00
_ HOW TO IMPROVE YOUR RACQUETBALL *Lubarsky Kaufman & Scagnetti*	5.00
_ HOW TO WIN AT POCKET BILLIARDS *Edward D. Knuchell*	5.00
_ JOY OF WALKING *Jack Scagnetti*	3.00
_ LEARNING & TEACHING SOCCER SKILLS *Eric Worthington*	3.00
_ MOTORCYCLING FOR BEGINNERS *I. G. Edmonds*	3.00
_ RACQUETBALL FOR WOMEN *Toni Hudson, Jack Scagnetti & Vince Rondone*	3.00
_ RACQUETBALL MADE EASY *Steve Lubarsky, Rod Delson & Jack Scagnetti*	5.00
_ SECRET OF BOWLING STRIKES *Dawson Taylor*	5.00
_ SECRET OF PERFECT PUTTING *Horton Smith & Dawson Taylor*	5.00
_ SOCCER—The Game & How to Play It *Gary Rosenthal*	5.00
_ STARTING SOCCER *Edward F. Dolan, Jr.*	3.00

TENNIS LOVERS' LIBRARY

_ BEGINNER'S GUIDE TO WINNING TENNIS *Helen Hull Jacobs*	2.00
_ HOW TO BEAT BETTER TENNIS PLAYERS *Loring Fiske*	4.00
_ HOW TO IMPROVE YOUR TENNIS—Style, Strategy & Analysis *C. Wilson*	2.00
_ PSYCH YOURSELF TO BETTER TENNIS *Dr. Walter A. Luszki*	2.00
_ TENNIS FOR BEGINNERS *Dr. H. A. Murray*	2.00
_ TENNIS MADE EASY *Joel Brecheen*	4.00
_ WEEKEND TENNIS—How to Have Fun & Win at the Same Time *Bill Talbert*	3.00
_ WINNING WITH PERCENTAGE TENNIS—Smart Strategy *Jack Lowe*	2.00

WILSHIRE PET LIBRARY

_ DOG OBEDIENCE TRAINING *Gust Kessopulos*	5.00
_ DOG TRAINING MADE EASY & FUN *John W. Kellogg*	4.00
_ HOW TO BRING UP YOUR PET DOG *Kurt Unkelbach*	2.00
_ HOW TO RAISE & TRAIN YOUR PUPPY *Jeff Griffen*	5.00

*The books listed above can be obtained from your book dealer or directly from
Melvin Powers. When ordering, please remit $1.00 postage for the first book
and 50¢ for each additional book.*

Melvin Powers
12015 Sherman Road, No. Hollywood, California 91605

WILSHIRE HORSE LOVERS' LIBRARY

*The books listed above can be obtained from your book dealer or directly from
Melvin Powers. When ordering, please remit $1.00 postage for the first book
and 50¢ for each additional book.*

Melvin Powers

12015 Sherman Road, No. Hollywood, California 91605

Melvin Powers' Favorite Books
HOW TO GET RICH IN MAIL ORDER
by Melvin Powers

Contents:
1. How to Develop Your Mail Order Expertise 2. How to Find a Unique Product or Service to Sell 3. How to Make Money with Classified Ads 4. How to Make Money with Display Ads 5. The Unlimited Potential for Making Money with Direct Mail 6. How to Copycat Successful Mail Order Operations 7. How I Created A Best Seller Using the Copycat Technique 8. How to Start and Run a Profitable Mail Order, Special Interest Book or Record Business 9. I Enjoy Selling Books by Mail—Some of My Successful and Not-So-Successful Ads and Direct Mail Circulars 10. Five of My Most Successful Direct Mail Pieces That Sold and Are Still Selling Millions of Dollars Worth of Books 11. Melvin Powers' Mail Order Success Strategy—Follow It and You'll Become a Millionaire 12. How to Sell Your Products to Mail Order Companies, Retail Outlets, Jobbers, and Fund Raisers for Maximum Distribution and Profits 13. How to Get Free Display Ads and Publicity That Can Put You on the Road to Riches 14. How to Make Your Advertising Copy Sizzle to Make You Wealthy 15. Questions and Answers to Help You Get Started Making Money in Your Own Mail Order Business 16. A Personal Word from Melvin Powers   **8½" x 11" — 352 Pages . . . $21 postpaid**

HOW TO SELF-PUBLISH YOUR BOOK AND HAVE THE FUN AND EXCITEMENT OF BEING A BEST-SELLING AUTHOR
by Melvin Powers

An expert's step-by-step guide to marketing your book successfully

176 Pages . . . $11.00 postpaid

A NEW GUIDE TO RATIONAL LIVING
by Albert Ellis, Ph.D. & Robert A. Harper, Ph.D.

Contents:
1. How Far Can You Go With Self-Analysis? 2. You Feel the Way You Think 3. Feeling Well by Thinking Straight 4. How You Create Your Feelings 5. Thinking Yourself Out of Emotional Disturbances 6. Recognizing and Attacking Neurotic Behavior 7. Overcoming the Influences of the Past 8. Does Reason Always Prove Reasonable? 9. Refusing to Feel Desperately Unhappy 10. Tackling Dire Needs for Approval 11. Eradicating Dire Fears of Failure 12. How to Stop Blaming and Start Living 13. How to Feel Undepressed though Frustrated 14. Controlling Your Own Destiny 15. Conquering Anxiety

256 Pages . . . $3.50 postpaid

PSYCHO-CYBERNETICS
A New Technique for Using Your Subconscious Power
by Maxwell Maltz, M.D., F.I.C.S.

Contents:
1. The Self Image: Your Key to a Better Life 2. Discovering the Success Mechanism Within You 3. Imagination—The First Key to Your Success Mechanism 4. Dehypnotize Yourself from False Beliefs 5. How to Utilize the Power of Rational Thinking 6. Relax and Let Your Success Mechanism Work for You 7. You Can Acquire the Habit of Happiness 8. Ingredients of the Success-Type Personality and How to Acquire Them 9. The Failure Mechanism: How to Make It Work For You Instead of Against You 10. How to Remove Emotional Scars, or How to Give Yourself an Emotional Face Lift 11. How to Unlock Your Real Personality 12. Do-It-Yourself Tranquilizers   **288 Pages . . . $5.50 postpaid**

A PRACTICAL GUIDE TO SELF-HYPNOSIS
by Melvin Powers

Contents:
1. What You Should Know About Self-Hypnosis 2. What About the Dangers of Hypnosis? 3. Is Hypnosis the Answer? 4. How Does Self-Hypnosis Work? 5. How to Arouse Yourself from the Self-Hypnotic State 6. How to Attain Self-Hypnosis 7. Deepening the Self-Hypnotic State 8. What You Should Know About Becoming an Excellent Subject 9. Techniques for Reaching the Somnambulistic State 10. A New Approach to Self-Hypnosis When All Else Fails 11. Psychological Aids and Their Function 12. The Nature of Hypnosis 13. Practical Applications of Self-Hypnosis   **128 Pages . . . $3.50 postpaid**

The books listed above can be obtained from your book dealer or directly from Melvin Powers.

Melvin Powers
12015 Sherman Road, No. Hollywood, California 91605

Notes

P. 33. the subconcious does not analyze, doubt, question

Notes

Notes

Notes

Notes